MANIFESTO FOR AMERICANS

MANIFESTO FOR AMERICANS

HARRY A. BULLIS

former Chairman of the Board,
General Mills, Inc.

McGRAW-HILL BOOK COMPANY, INC.

New York   Toronto   London

MANIFESTO FOR AMERICANS

To my wonderful mother,
who radiated the spirit
of the America I love, and
the world I want to live in

ACKNOWLEDGMENTS

In the preparation of this book I acknowledge gratefully the assistance of Dwight Cooke, Dr. Arthur R. Upgren, S. Marshall Kempner, Marcus P. Stark, Harold I. Lunde and Robert J. Blakely.

I appreciate the great inspiration and encouragement I have received from my wife, Maria.

To these and to all the others who have given me help and inspiration I express my sincere gratitude and appreciation.

Harry A. Bullis

CONTENTS

MANIFESTO FOR AMERICANS

A BUSINESSMAN'S CREDO

NO AMERICAN is born with a full appreciation of his country, just as no human being is born with an understanding of the inner drives that will impel him all through his life or with a ready-made set of goals toward which he will strive. Goals and understanding, perception and maturity are matters that evolve and emerge—and that must be worked at, by men and by nations.

In this life and on the earth as we know it, we shall never have all the answers. But, if we seek earnestly we can find some of them. We need a good many answers in these days; we must spend our energy to continue finding them. Our century, for us as individuals and for the United States as a nation, is a time in which change has accelerated and challenge has intensified more than ever before in any comparable span of recorded history.

Americans today—all of us—must re-examine our situation and re-evaluate our beliefs and our actions. We must be somewhat like the Roman god who could look both directions at once: we must remain aware of the notable development of our past; we must concentrate on the future; and at the same moment we must continue to produce at maximum efficiency in our chosen fields of endeavor.

In regarding both past and present, we must reraise a kind of spiritual banner—a standard beneath which a humanity that now numbers three billion living souls can live and progress.

Since I have learned through many years that we can profit

3

from the experience and thoughts of others if we will, I have written this book as my legacy and my credo. It cannot give even all the answers I should like it to give, but it can give some; it will raise questions and it can help in redefining the kind of standard we must raise and support if we are long to survive. Some of my strong and long-held convictions I shall mention in this section. Others that have sustained me personally throughout my life emerge in following chapters. I venture to offer them because I believe they are vital to us today and because I believe that many other people share them, at least intuitively.

I BELIEVE, for example, that *freedom is indivisible*. It is impossible to preserve our political freedom if economic freedom is suppressed—whether for capital's benefit by irresponsible profit-taking or for labor's benefit by irresponsible and wasteful work rules, or for the state's convenience by confiscatory taxes and unreasonable government controls. No people can long benefit from economic freedom if they tolerate infringements on any of the other rights of men, whether the restrictions be upon religious liberty, political freedom, freedom of thought and expression, freedom from racial discrimination, or the right of any individual to move freely to whatever position in society his own endowments and energies entitle him.

If we ever part with even a small portion of any one of our freedoms, we may fall into the abyss of dictatorship and destruction. We must be vigilant to preserve freedom. The protection, harmonizing, and responsible exercise of all our freedoms all of the time must be our prime concern as individuals and collectively as a nation. Our freedom must always include government by the consent of the governed, economic production and distribution by free workers and consumers, intellectual and artistic expression limited only by the abilities of men to communicate, and religious experience limited only by the dictates

of conscience and heart. Let one freedom fail and all are en-
dangered.

I believe that life requires an *enthusiastic hospitality to new
ideas and to innovation, whether popular or unpopular.* Francis
Bacon said "He that will not apply new remedies must expect
new evils; for time is the greatest innovator." Having long ad-
mired the lives of the great inventors and innovators, I have
tried to indicate in this book some of the opportunities daily offered to each of us to bring about constructive change and
progress in our lives and in the world. As individuals and as a
nation, we are today part of a swiftly changing world in which
glittering generalities and high-sounding ideals handed down
from the past are not enough. We must indeed preserve our
great heritage of freedom, but we best preserve it when we are
receptive to new ideas and fresh points of view. Americans must
tirelessly search for fresh political formulas and better economic
programs. Only if we constantly re-examine our own bases criti-
cally and enthusiastically welcome new ideas can we move forward on the tides of the future instead of being overwhelmed by
them.

I believe in *accentuating the positive.* When I was a mill employee with the old Washburn Crosby Company I adopted the
motto that still hangs on the wall of my office: *Drive Straight
Ahead with a Positive Mental Attitude.* My positive inclinations
are a consequence of my religious convictions. I believe that we
can each have a part in shaping our future by dedicating our
lives to the Creator. A man cannot be tough-minded and con-
fident without faith in himself which he gets from faith in God.
There is so much confusion in our hearts and minds today that
we must stop and listen for wisdom from an infinite source.

To me, "positive thinking" means thought that moves forward
through problems until a conclusion or judgment can be reached.
This in turn produces a course of action which should then be

pursued relentlessly and with complete confidence that it will lead to the right results.

Unfortunately, there has developed in our country a trend to "play it safe" and to be satisfied with a little security rather than take risks that might bring great returns in personal satisfaction, social gain, or national progress. We forget in so doing that the position of leadership we hold in the world today was built upon a foundation of optimism and self-confidence—positive thinking, as I am using it here—not pessimism.

There are many ways to define success. I think it is fair to say a human being is a success when he uses life well and contributes something good to his fellows; when he leaves behind him no residue of unhappiness, no dissipated energy or undeveloped talent, and when he thus achieves for himself inner peace and deep satisfaction.

Any formula for individual success begins and ends with personal enterprise. It includes, too, the fact that when you help the other fellow get ahead you are helping yourself. The rules are few but potent. To anyone searching for success I would say: Establish your goals. Fire yourself with enthusiasm and positive thinking. Strive to serve first and seek reward second. Begin and end your career with a concern for others.

In these days, for true success, we must also avoid the easy road of conformity for conformity's sake. As citizens of a free society, we should be sympathetic to new ideas and new policies at home and abroad, particularly to those policies that bring successful progress and growth. Progress furnishes the only ultimate solution to the complex problems of our time. Yet consider how often people cling to the *status-quo* or don't-rock-the-boat view of the world in which they live. We must keep our mental processes alive and growing. Otherwise, both we and our country will become stagnant and ultimately we shall fail.

More of us must become tough-minded if we are to succeed today. Tough-mindedness is an evidence of spiritual optimism, of self-respect and a belief in order and progress. It is made up in part of a steadfast conviction that God is an orderly God, not a capricious force, and that God wants men and women to live full, spiritually successful, and satisfying lives.

The ideas of freedom, the dignity of man, and the sanctity of the individual grow directly out of deeply rooted religious principles and convictions. The lives of countless human beings and leaders of men—throughout history—give evidence of guidance by an intelligence of a spiritual nature. Surely the men who wrote the Declaration of Independence and the Constitution of the United States were sustained by something beyond human inspiration. When we think of man's struggle with the world about him, we can remember the moral courage of Abraham Lincoln and the unflinching strength he drew from his faith.

The religious man is constantly being illuminated and energized by God. Man, by shaping his nature to the pattern revealed by the Creator, builds and strengthens a relationship through which universal and creative energy flows to him.

Religion to me is a deeply personal and moving force. Whenever I have to make a vital decision, or solve some problem that will affect not only my personal life but also the lives of people who work with me or depend on my judgment, I trust my own intelligence and experience only up to a point. Beyond that I am humble. I pray daily for guidance, and follow what I believe to be God's prompting.

I AM GENUINELY OPTIMISTIC about our future, despite the tumult of present conditions in the world. My optimism is not the result of wishful thinking. It has the toughest core any philosophy can possibly have: all my life I have believed in God. I have always found that the men whose attitudes and outlooks were positive and who had the most confidence in themselves and in the future had religious faith.

And I believe in America. My belief in our country is ultimately based upon the great potentialities of our citizens who —with increasing knowledge and greater realization of our resources—are renewing their faith in our traditions and principles and are pursuing great and positive goals not only within our borders but throughout the world.

HARRY A. BULLIS

Minneapolis, Minnesota

ONE

CHANGE AND CHALLENGE

NEVER BEFORE in history has any nation been so profoundly challenged as the United States of America is today. We are challenged by the Soviet Union in the exploration of new worlds beyond our own. Nearer at hand, we are confronted with the growing economic, political, and military intention of Moscow and Peking expressly to "bury capitalism." The most urgent challenge and greatest opportunity we face is to make a better life for our children and to help billions of people seeking a better life in foreign and underdeveloped lands to help themselves.

The acceleration of change in human events is part of virtually every man's experience today. Portions of the world that were once part of vast colonial empires are gaining their independence; new nations are being formed at an astonishing rate. The United Nations has grown from fifty-two to ninety-nine members, and a dozen more are on the way. Scientific discoveries continue at an increasing pace in the highly developed countries, but the people of many of the newest nations are centuries behind us in the discovery and application of science as we now know it to the production even of the basic economic necessities. Not sufficiency, not plenty, but poverty and hunger are the customary mode of life for two thirds of the world's population. Most of the new nations also lack experience in self-government and law, and there is among them a notable lack of education and training for sound economic and social progress. Yet these peoples are beginning to learn that a better life is pos-

9

sible. The wonders of modern communication now enable them to see what the more fortunate nations enjoy—sometimes, sadly enough, in a superficial or distorted picture. They are ambitious and impatient; they want to catch up in a hurry; they want to partake of the benefits and pleasures of modern industrial technology. The "revolution of rising expectations" has become a "revolution of rising demands." Now people are expecting and demanding a better life for themselves and for their children.

Actual and enduring world peace will become possible only as we narrow the chasm between the poor nations and the rich, and as we make far more widely available to all citizens the standards for daily living which are the visible fruits of the best free-enterprise systems. Americans particularly, as members of a free society, are faced with the urgent necessity of learning how to help these underdeveloped people to help themselves without delay; how realistically to aid them in raising their living standards; how to help them understand what workable democracy means and to make them self-sustaining and contributing members of a world that is in fact free. For our own good —if there were no other reasons—we cannot turn away from this heavy responsibility. Peace and continued prosperity in America will not come from isolation. It is to the national interest of the United States and other advanced countries to speed up the development of the poorer countries. Such assistance from advanced countries to less developed countries is not an act of charity; it is the right and realistic thing to do to help the poor develop their own potentialities and it is an intelligent way for the donor nations to strengthen their own economies. No countries should be more interested in an expanding economy than the advanced countries, not only in their own territories but throughout the world. An expanding world economy is an essential goal for every advanced country. It is now necessary for the survival of our way of life that the world's new nations learn to live in the family of nations, recognizing in terms of action the dignity of man and not looking to war as a means of gaining their immediate or long-term goals.

Even if they do not clamor at our consciences or disturb our sleep in comfortable beds, the desperate needs of the human beings who seek bread and dignity jeopardize our own security until those needs are met. This problem is made far more urgent by another great change in our time—the emergence of a dead-earnest competitor. The Communists too are striving to win these hungry people. In fewer than fifty years Russia has changed from a Czarist dictatorship—through Lenin's experimentation, through Stalin's purges—into Khrushchev's present interpretation of communism through imperialism and tyranny. And in Asia other Communists are indoctrinating the Chinese with Mao's version of Marxian socialism. Unfortunately for the way of freedom as we conceive it, the intense dedication of these Communists is showing marked results. Russia continues to make material progress. China is developing a functioning science and technology; she is building her military strength, increasing her industrial power, and advancing in the direction of nuclear energy and the hydrogen bomb. China is determined to become one of the great economic as well as political powers of the twentieth-century world.

Between the conflicting ideological centers of East and West are an Africa and Asia in foment and a rapidly changing South America. Thus far, the majority of South Asians and Africans have shown little desire to be either communized or American-ized. Recently separated from European colonialism, these new nations by and large want to shape their own destinies in free-dom. If they can solve their problems of poverty, illiteracy, disease, and racial and social discrimination speedily within the frame of reference of a free society, they can permanently resist Communist imperialism. In helping these peoples to grow and to help themselves in a stable and expanding international economy lies our greatest opportunity.

Between 1950 and 1960 the Western nations have raised their per capita income significantly, to record heights of affluence. During the same ten years, the poor nations have improved their lot only a little. Certainly we cannot hope to win these peoples for freedom and stop the encroachment of communism if we allow them to remain hungry, diseased, and undereducated.

Whether we Americans like it or not, we are in a critical struggle with Moscow and Peking for world leadership. For our survival and the survival of the free world we must shoulder the responsibility for the economic, political, and moral destiny of two thirds of mankind. Every free and every uncommitted nation looks to the United States for leadership. The state of the world of the future depends on what they find.

We must keep faith in ourselves and our traditions. The brotherhood of man is more than a cliché: it is a necessity. We must sacrifice whatever is necessary to extend our basic ideology and to implement our ethics by applying our productive skills and American know-how here and elsewhere to raise the living standards of *all* the peoples of the world. Above all, we must actively realize that only through an internally strong America can we hope to have our counsels prevail beyond our borders.

We have many problems on the home front, many areas in which hard-headed re-evaluation is required. One of the things that is right about America is that we can say when and where we are wrong. We are wrong when we are unable or unwilling to face up to racial and religious intolerance. We are wrong in our individual reluctance to do more than is barely necessary for the world community. We are wrong when we resist supporting better educational programs for our own children. We are wrong if we become so swamped in our advantages of growing wealth and comfortable living that except for the purposes of self-defense and self-interest we lack the vision and the good will to move with positive action to assist the less fortunate in underdeveloped lands and to lead in the tremendous task of world reconstruction. When we admit we are wrong we have taken the first step forward in improvement, and we are ready to move on.

What can be done?

First, we must make our economy as effective as possible by eliminating waste and inefficiency in government, industry, and labor. We must keep that economy operating close to its full productive capacity. We must resist rising costs and inflation by stimulating technological advance and by the most effective use of our power to produce. We must stay active and move ahead in all these areas to keep our home base strong and prosperous. We must preserve and enlarge the great productive power that is ours, thus maintaining our defenses and beginning to assume the tremendous responsibilities we have because we are the nation we have become since 1776.

Second, we must work in constantly closer cooperation with all the countries of the free world. This entails strengthening our military, economic, and cultural ties with those older nations whose traditions and ideals are in general harmony with ours— and with those new nations for whom we seek freedom on their terms. The economic and political problems of the world can be solved if the massed forces of the free world, both in the well developed and the less developed nations, are mobilized to counteract the menace of Communist domination.

Our fundamental purpose must be to lead the other nations of our world in an all-out campaign against human want, illiteracy, and misery. We can continue to serve—but we can serve better—the needs of vast numbers of people in South America, in the Middle East, in Africa, and in Asia by helping them to help themselves.

When technical assistance is called for, we can recruit from our great corporations the best managerial talent for efficient production. We can recruit the best engineers and craftsmen to work with and to teach local workers to build the roads, airstrips, schools, power plants, and factories that are so sorely needed. We can recruit American agricultural experts to train the farmers in underdeveloped lands. Political scientists and skilled government workers can be made available to train newly independent people in the fine art of governing themselves. Teachers can teach teachers. Expert women can teach local women domestic science and home improvement for an immediately better life. Physicians and nurses can train their counterparts in the prevention and control of disease. Aid by teaching and training can materially and rapidly bring about self-reliance and lay the foundation for ongoing improvement on the part of those who must now realistically be judged "less fortunate." For significant and durable results, however, the beneficiaries must learn to do for themselves, for no one but they can bring about the ultimate development of their country. These countries must have good leadership and the citizens must do their part in working intelligently and supporting development projects.

Technical assistance is not a totally new concept. The United States, for instance, has been doing this on a small scale for a number of years. Now the time has come to go to work on a world-wide scale, although the program should not be the exclusive endeavor of any one nation. Every nation can—and should be willing to—supply trained personnel for this highly desirable warfare, the war against want and injustice.

In most underdeveloped countries, many people can neither read nor write and there has been very little secondary education. In these countries, secondary and technical education must be built up and encouraged and there must be developed balanced programs of education which are geared into the economic progress these countries are attempting to achieve. The present need is for more trained farmers and efficient technicians who will increase the production of economic goods. People are these countries' greatest resources; better utilization should be made of them. Many leaders must be trained from the middle-level class before the people will move from poverty to a comfortable type of living. To start and carry on such educational programs will require competent and dedicated teachers from the advanced countries, working in cooperation with the United Nations and other agencies.

Such a balanced assistance program to speed up the development of the poorer nations will demand some sacrifice from the people of every country. To work, it will cost a large amount of money—but that cost would be only a minute fraction of the cost of a nuclear holocaust. It will take years, perhaps generations, to accomplish. But waging peace on a grand scale will release that energetic imagination now only waiting direction, and real results will appear. Our own country's prosperity will gain, and the economic growth of every nation that participates will be enhanced. It will bring to life in the world of today the principles for which our forefathers fought in the American War for Independence—the principles of equity, of justice, and of opportunity—and these principles will be rededicated even more widely.

We Americans possess enormous strength. Every worthy struggle and every good action of man rises from a spiritual base: the good for which he strives, the service for which he lives. In the American concept of human dignity and freedom, in our belief in the divine right of each individual to grow to his full potential and to develop his God-given capacities, we have a compass that can show us—and the world—the way. We can demonstrate that our sustained and constructive effort of economic assistance has for its goal not the exploitation of under-developed peoples but the development of their own potential-ities for their own good.

In the meantime, is there any hope that a nuclear war can be avoided while these economic, political, and social changes are taking place across the globe and while a fairer and more ample world is being built? If we mobilize competent-plus persons in science, education, politics, industry, labor, religion, and the arts to work creatively and courageously—and *now*—on world problems, there is good reason to believe that we can. But we must act. We must have a true sense of urgency. Today a good foreign policy comes from the possession of a fast-moving do-mestic economy and a strong fortress at home. My conviction is that there is no "inevitable" war ahead if Americans wake up. If we take the positive approach; if we maintain our vision and our traditional purpose to build a good society; if we revitalize our entire economy and put our best knowledge to work; if we modernize our armed might; if we extend and improve our ed-ucational system; and if we realize that we ourselves hold the power to control our destiny within sufficiently wide limits to allow us successfully to meet the challenges we face, we shall not fail.

Our survival today depends on power. But what does *power* mean in terms of economics, education, and research, in terms of the amount of capital invested in our plants and all the other things that make for high productivity? Above all, what does it mean in terms of the spirit—in ideas, the dignity of man and the preservation of his individual rights and freedoms? We must not forget that the most important aspect of the struggle we are now engaged in is for men's minds. The power of any state sys-tem rests in what it can do for its people and how it helps its people do for themselves. As Americans we must never be ashamed of the record of our system, and it behooves us to be informed and ready to tell others about it. Most of all, in our time of change and challenge we will have to *use* our power, and use it wisely. Our survival and that of the world we believe in depends on its intelligent use and on whether we can continue to express by constructive action our real and deep concern for the people of other lands and to lead in creating a new world of opportunity for the whole family of man.

TWO

FREE ECONOMY AND STABILITY

THE AMERICAN ECONOMY is a uniquely workable system of free enterprise by means of which our resources are transformed into products and services of worth to mankind. It is a free economy that furnishes and safeguards maximum opportunities for individuals to produce and prosper. It is one in which productivity, purchasing power, research, and capital investment are lifegiving elements.

Economics is one of the subjects to which professional students devote lifetimes of thought and discussion. The total library of books on the subject is much more extensive today than is a collection of the world's enduring classics of literature. Even with all this, one sometimes feels that a clear-cut and satisfactory definition of the economic system of the United States has not yet been arrived at, and that this reasonably healthy economic organism of ours is a tremendously complex thing.

Our economy *is* complex, but this fact is no justification for any of us to keep from understanding as much as possible about it and doing what we can to contribute to its continued health and stability.

Economic and political commentators throughout our country's history have frequently viewed our system with wide-eyed alarm, although it has not foundered even in the darkest days of depression and financial panic. At the other extreme, a great many people in the country have taken a complacent attitude that could be summed up by saying: "Well, it works. Therefore there's no need to think about it; there is nothing wrong with it."

In view of the vastness and complexity of our country's economy today, I do not want to imply that—even in the longest chapter in a short book—anyone could solve all the problems, actual or possible, in the economic picture, or even raise all the questions that could be considered to advantage. I am not by any means attempting to make a study in full and scholarly depth. But I do believe that there are certain points that should be brought up about our economy and its stability, today and for the future.

OUR ECONOMY is the sum of the productive activity of our total population. It requires all our professional skills. This economic organism is fed by capital; through its arterial system courses the money supply; its end products are goods and services. But it is not an automatic organism; it functions only because it can utilize the brains and the imagination and labor of many millions of gainfully employed citizens.

None of us (the experts included) is fully certain of its exact requirements for permanence and optimum vitality. Certainly it will not function long if the laws of supply and demand do not set prices, and most certainly a climate of freedom is essential to its life. Liberty based on moral law is a spiritual ingredient without which it will eventually decay. When the laws of supply and demand are not allowed to operate freely, some other authority must dominate these fields of decision. That produces an authoritarian government or economic order. Someone then must *dictate*.

Today our economy is powerfully affected by other systems on other continents; no longer can it be contained within the safe vacuum of our national boundaries. Even fifty years ago it was a relatively simple and self-contained domestic matter; now, whether we like it or not, ours has become a complex and world economy. The long-term domestic prosperity of the United States is directly related to our ability to assist the creation of dynamic and expanding economies throughout the rest of the inhabited world—free and functioning economies, not mere carbon copies of our own in areas in which different conditions prevail. But the building and strengthening of other free nations will not "just happen" in the regular course of events. We must work at it—as other peoples must—with understanding and courage and the willingness to risk.

After all, American institutions have never been only a casual mixture of wild ideologies and assorted daydreams. We have a sturdy lineage; in its best aspects our country is the child of the union of personal freedom under law with free enterprise. Today we willingly—sometimes even greedily—accept the fruits of our economic system, but too many of us have not taken the trouble to get as clear an idea as possible of how the system works or why it has been so remarkably successful. Too few of us are even aware how inseparably interlocked are freedom of the individual and freedom of enterprise—and too few appear to know that this fusion is the keystone of the structure.

The nation's founders set up a political and economic basis for the new Republic that fused many elements of the old orders into a new entity, much as a horticulturist grafts tender shoots onto a strong young stalk. Anyone who knows anything of the history of that period knows that the Founding Fathers did not go about this haphazardly. Business freedom has now grown so completely together with the concept and practice of personal liberty that one cannot be attacked without threatening the other.

Today a free market and an industry that takes full advantage of scientific and technological achievements furnish the only secure guarantee that our high standard of living will continue. Competition, which is the essence of a free market, is the constant spur for better know-how and efficiency. A free market guarantees that we will use the best of all available techniques and constantly, through science and research, seek a better way of doing things. A free market is the *only* impartial purveyor of products to all elements in our society. More than that, the modern free market is the best device man has yet developed for the voluntary coordination of human economic effort: it channels that effort into the areas of greatest need and governs production and distribution accordingly.

Another basic truth about our economic system is this: It combines stability and dynamic progress in a way of life that allows maximum freedom under law. So long as we have this freedom, change of every description can evolve creatively to continue progress. Sound ideas thrive in the air of freedom; unsound ideas, exposed to critical examination, are quickly seen for what they are.

During the Middle Ages, the conduct of merchants and craftsmen was closely regulated. The guild system was a healthy and necessary stage of development in the history of commerce, but its restrictions choked many new techniques and methods, and discouraged progress. With the first real impact of the industrial revolution came the realization that freedom of individual enterprise fosters progress. The last vestiges of the medieval guilds began to disappear. Translated into both the political and the economic spheres, the principles of freedom operating through the free-enterprise system have given the Western nations more than a century of advancement that has eclipsed the combined mercantile gains of the dozen preceding centuries.

FROM THE BEGINNING, the material progress we have achieved in America has been animated by the profit system. This predicates that each individual has complete freedom to choose his own way of making a living. This is part of each American's birthright.

Ours is a system in which production is governed by prices that permit the producer to realize a profit. Striving for profit is thus a basic motivating force—and, in some instances, it has been overdone. The profit is not the end objective of our free-enterprise system. Our objective, stated in the Preamble to the United States Constitution, is "to advance the general welfare." Profit is just a mechanism to this end. In a search to enlarge its profit—in which business has had only one billion dollars of success in the past ten years—business has performed yeoman service as the greatest single contributing force, to more than a hundred-billion-dollar enlargement of the "compensation of labor."

But the profit motive by itself is not enough to assure a healthy free enterprise. Another underlying force in our system is the satisfaction of creating better goods and furnishing better services. To win lasting success in a free economy the two must go together; competition is intense in the open market, and the consumer turns to the products that serve him best at prices he can pay. It is the business system seeking profit which actually *creates* the income of the workers which they use to buy the products of their efforts. To a large extent as a result of the working of the profit system, scientific discoveries relating to industry have followed one another with amazing speed; technical progress has been correspondingly rapid—an interaction of economy and technology made possible by the use of accumulated capital. The search by these means to try to enlarge profits is what actually enlarges the workers' welfare. As business grows, improves, and expands, it must hire workers. To do so it bids for them. This is the process which has so greatly increased U.S. workers' incomes.

No businessman has a mandate from heaven. We *earn* our opportunities in this world. Under the profit-and-loss system, those who serve best have the best chance for survival—and production generally stays longest in the hands of the most efficient.

WITH THE PROFIT MOTIVE in mind, let us remember that—whatever our field of endeavor—each of us has an economic and political duty to help keep our nation's economy reasonably well in balance. In business, the best way to do this is to strive constantly for maximum output at minimum cost. *Maximum output* means the best possible use of labor, equipment, and material; *minimum cost* means constant effort to avoid waste, overcome inefficiency, and utilize production techniques and tools that will lower costs.

Business cannot help keep our economy in balance unless it makes good use of every dollar in the sales total. Every dollar must be put to work to generate income for someone. In the sixteen years since the end of World War II, total business paid out to all income-receiving groups more dollars than the total dollars business got from the sale of all of its output. Because business has expanded, it has borrowed this excess of dollars to pay as income to its own workers, to the workers who produce all the materials and supplies business buys, and to all other income-receiving groups, including government.

Large profits should not be hoarded as cash; this cuts down the flow of dollars. All earnings should be put to work for the benefit of society. One way of doing this is by expanding production facilities to produce more goods and by installing equipment that will turn out those goods at a lower cost per unit. Increased efficiency in turn means more product per man-hour of labor—the sound basis for higher wages and living standards.

When organized labor gains higher money wages, for a time costs rise. This in turn should provide additional incentive to the businessman to use more or better equipment to reduce the cost of wages per unit of output by expanding the number of units produced per man-hour of work.

Productivity is a term rather often bandied about today by popular commentators who turn out to have less than a full understanding of its implications. One simple gauge and definition of productivity was given in the preceding paragraph: the number of units produced per man per hour in our industry. Increased productivity is the sole key to economic growth and well-being. Clearly, unless more is produced, there is no more in which to share. There are three primary ways to increase productivity: (1) Upgrading worker effectiveness by better training programs. (2) Application of improved methods and machines to work problems. (3) Expansion of production capacity through increased capital investment.

Each of these methods interacts with the others, and management has the task of convincing workers that increased productivity is in their own self-interest: as they produce more, they will be able to buy more because real wages will be higher. Management obviously cannot get this truth across to workers if selfish or misguided union leaders continue to agitate for more pay in return for equal or less production. Cooperation is necessary, with some flexibility on both sides, but essential economic principles cannot be defied. Such an economic absurdity as more pay for less product can only propel labor and capital toward an economic smash-up.

Responsible people in all walks of life—the professions, labor, management, and agriculture—must awake and also dispel the mirage of the fairy-godmother state, a fallacy based on the same something-for-nothing premise. If workers get more pay but produce no more, there is no gain for anybody—least of all for the workers. The only route to greater national and individual wealth is more and more productivity—something business can do more than merely talk about. Given reasoned cooperation from government and labor, business can continue to deliver the goods—with full fairness to the employee. It has demonstrated this again and again.

There are other reasons we should all try to bend the productivity curve upward. We need more goods for an increasing population, a population that includes a rising proportion of the retired and the aged. People who live on fixed incomes are the ones who suffer most from wage inflation. We need more real and effective wealth to provide for them and still maintain present living standards, as well as about a million *new* jobs every year to employ our expanding labor force.

Maintenance of full employment is one of our foremost domestic challenges. Business and government must indeed work together to accomplish this, but full employment must not be considered primarily the responsibility of government. Unless national defense raises the figure, government should not be expected to provide as much as 10 per cent of total employment in any year. The jobs, if our economy is to stay free, must be provided by private industry—not merely the great enterprises but also small business, agriculture, and the service industries.

Clearly, only business can provide the jobs which will be demanded in the American economy. This lesson remained almost completely unlearned in the decade of the 1930s. Present political leadership has given evidence that it thoroughly appreciates that the largest amount of jobs must flow in from business and, therefore, all groups must encourage business by tax reduction and in other ways. Giving these incentives means giving more jobs at better pay to workers; it does not mean giving any handouts to business. Competition of business will accomplish precisely this result, as it has during the past sixteen years. Those years were indeed favorable to business, but by far the largest share of the reward flowed to labor.

Business can provide new jobs by increasing production, but in doing this businessmen will at the same time have to direct tremendous initiative to keeping more goods moving at realistic prices. It is a law of economic life that the American standard of living will continue to stay high *only* if we can make more and more goods available at prices people can afford to pay.

As a corollary to increased production, increased earnings reward those who serve the public by furnishing most efficiently what it needs and wants. Monetary reward remains the best incentive to a better job and is a motivation that operates equally among people in factory and office, salesmen in the field, the executives who do the planning, and the owners who furnish plants and tools.

I have already pointed out that the effects of American productivity extend far beyond our national borders. In the second half of the twentieth century they mean not only internal prosperity for our country; they also affect political direction and economic life for many other peoples. Whatever else it entails, the Cold War is the ultimate challenge to the American concept of expanded living standards—for all citizens—created by a free people engaged in free enterprise. As things now stand, the success of the United States in the Cold War will depend to a major extent upon our ability to prove to the rest of the world that private enterprise is able to give the people it serves a rising standard of living in a society that provides jobs for those who need them.

BY REALISTIC STANDARDS, the American economy can be judged to be strong. It must be kept strong by the people who benefit from it, and it cannot stand still; it must grow. Many economists agree that a minimum growth rate in the Gross National Product of 3 per cent a year is an absolute necessity to insure a continued strong economy.

Merely to keep up economically with the present growth rate of the population in the United States means that we must feed, clothe, house, and educate three million additional people each year. Add to that the human need for recreation, a justifiable desire for improvement in living standards for all, a larger percentage than ever before of our population over seventy, and the need to provide more self-development opportunities for both young and old—they indicate clearly that our Gross National Product must indeed increase every year.

These things are worth striving for, but they become virtually worthless if we cannot safeguard our free institutions. Thus an overpowering reason for insuring that our economy stays strong is the fact that it is the basis of our national security and one of the predicates of our status of international leadership. The cost of security, in terms of military strength alone, is about one tenth of our Gross National Product. Until we come closer to the goal of one world, these costs are more likely to rise than to decline; if our economy gains strength and our production increases, the burden will be more bearable.

In the Korean effort we spent ten billion dollars more for defense than we are spending today. In the ensuing years total production has increased by more than 50 per cent. Thus we are able clearly to manage a greater defense program and greater aid to less developed areas. Moreover, of this recent gain in production, only a very minor fraction reflects rising prices. It is significant to note that the wholesale price level in March 1961 was no higher than in March 1951.

Our security is now interwoven with the development of the rest of the free world. Our economy can never again be considered merely an instrument for the good of our own national society alone. If it is to survive, it must afford the material means of giving hope and a new kind of life to the less fortunate peoples of the world, and it must begin effectively to do this quickly. Our economy furnishes the wherewithal both for our security and our own pursuit of happiness, but unless others are allowed —and assisted—to develop their own, our happiness is threatened and our security is diminished.

Enlightened American attention to the less fully developed areas of the world is a subject I shall deal with at greater length in another chapter. Suffice it to say here that our own self-interest requires immediate, hard-headed, well-managed efforts in this direction. In comparison to our tremendous resources, our international programs are still incredibly small. In the economic sphere, improved assistance includes a much larger flow of capital investment, skilled personnel, and trade.

ON THE DOMESTIC SCENE, businessmen must concern themselves with maintaining purchasing power at a high level and raising the living standards of the whole population, with particular concentration at present on aiding those groups whose living level is below the national standard—and this means better products at lower prices.

The challenge, then, is one of maintaining a satisfactory balance between production and consumption. The money paid out for plant facilities, machinery, raw materials, wages, and operating expenses must be brought back in the form of sales dollars the consumer pays because he wants or needs the goods or services produced, balanced by his ability to pay the prices charged. But sales dollars must include more than the total cost of goods or services plus a reasonable profit. They must ultimately furnish the capital for long-term growth and for investment in research, development of new methods, and expanded and improved facilities for production. The role of marketing in this period is more significant than at any previous time in our history. Effective marketing moves our production to its ultimate consumer quickly, efficiently, and at low cost.

THE TWO GREAT DRIVING FORCES in the American economy, certainly since the middle of the nineteenth century, have been innovation and investment. More and more in our time, these spring from research and development—and they are possible only because of the availability and expenditure of accumulated capital.

Our nation has gone through phases—a period of development of canals and river travel, for example; the period in which railroads united the expanding nation; and a continuous improvement in manufacturing techniques, a phase that began during the colonial period. Now we have reached the nuclear, electronic, and space period, with who knows what in store for the future.

At one stage of our development, inventions were often the result of chance (a prime example is the vulcanization of rubber) but today most of our new discoveries come from the research laboratories manned by teams of scientists and inventors. In many respects the glamour occupation of our time, research has produced enormous technological advance; it seems almost magic. In actual fact, industrial research is purposeful hard work, and many of the projects undertaken do not succeed.

We now live in a world the population of which is doubling about every half-century. We are faced with the practical challenge and spiritual necessity of feeding, housing, and employing this expanding population. The vastness of this problem is brought home when we realize that even today only a quarter of the world's population has an adequate diet, that another quarter is underfed, and the other half is constantly on the verge of starvation.

Scientists and industrialists in the world of the near future are going to be faced with the problem of furnishing raw materials to sustain this population—food; material for clothing and shelter; and the thousands of necessities for industry. Today, for instance, twenty tons of raw material come out of the earth each year for each person in the United States. With increasing needs, new materials and new sources will be required. In the past our sources of industrial energy have been coal, petroleum, and water power. Now we have also begun to seek in the rays of the sun and in nuclear energy other and eventually less costly sources.

THERE ARE TWO chief types of research: basic and applied. Basic research pursues new knowledge without regard to its immediate practical application. Applied research brings existing knowledge to bear on the development of new or improved products and processes.

Sir Alexander Fleming's discovery of penicillin was a by-product of his lifetime study of molds and fungi, and Sir William Ramsey's discovery of neon gas was certainly not motivated by the hope of inventing the neon sign. On the other hand, the contributions of applied research to modern life range—to name only a few—from the incandescent lamp and the reaper to instant cake mixes and ball-point pens.

Both types of research are essential to progress, and our future needs will require an ever-increasing number of scientists working on thousands of problems in every imaginable field to keep up with changing production and changing consumer tastes. The character of the modern world requires the modern businessman to be an innovator, and the future of any company is now linked with research.

INVENTION AND INNOVATION in industry—and therefore desirable growth and progress—are closely tied in a free economy to the investment of capital. Capital investment makes possible the new buildings and equipment for new and improved products. Investment is the means for maintaining inventories of raw materials and for the production of finished goods in the period before the sales dollars begin to come back. Investment is also made in the workers who must be trained to operate the machines and supervise the processes. Investment made in the workers and in the population in the form of training, skills, and education actually produces an investment return that probably compares favorably with the investment return on plant and equipment expansion. Very wisely, increased attention is being given to this investment in personnel, because ultimately the success of both our economic system and the well-being of our society depends upon a trained manpower.

Only 7 per cent of the world's population, Americans enjoy about 30 per cent of the world's output of consumable goods. The average cost of machinery available to each worker is about fifteen thousand dollars, with investment per worker in many industries (among them public utilities, oil, and chemicals) running several times this average.

The American scale of living in the future will depend to an important degree on the amount of capital per worker that continues to be invested in American industry. Our economy has been able to remain strong because our system has produced a marked step-up in the rate of capital formation, making possible an equivalent expansion of investment. The amount of money industry invests in tools and equipment for each worker directly affects his productivity. And as each worker's productivity increases cost per unit decreases, demand grows and consumption is stimulated, new jobs are created, and the over-all standard of living rises.

Thus the process that has brought such great abundance in America begins when business invests capital; then industry can produce and distribute more goods to consumers. If an automobile manufacturer, for instance, wishes to make more cars— more than the capacity of his present facilities—he must build an additional plant, buy machines, train more workers, and gather inventories of needed materials. Only then can he begin to produce the extra automobiles.

This entire process of capital accumulation and investment is a voluntary one in our free-market economy, and it is to a very large extent the consumer in the market place who dictates by his purchases what is to be produced. The possibility of profit for the worker and for capital stimulates both to improve services and products. Utilizing science and the benefits of research, with the motivation of making a reasonable amount of profit and a belief in the free-enterprise economy, capital is invested; the results are an ever-greater output per man-hour, a higher standard of living for all involved, and the possibility of sharing both materially and spiritually with those outside our borders.

What economists call "the marginal productivity of the worker" is increased as larger capital investment is made by business. Competition assures to the worker a wage which since World War II has certainly equaled, and in monetary wages has exceeded, this marginal productivity of labor.

IT SHOULD BE OBVIOUS that the basic support for this country's astoundingly high wage structure is the amount of capital that industry has invested to increase productivity. But *capital* is not a cold, purely selfish force or an evil genius personified, as the most outspoken enemies of our way of life attempt to picture it—thereby avoiding all issues except those that can be turned to their advantage. Our high wages, which mean high purchasing power, for instance, do not—cannot—result from undue restriction of the total number of workers or from limitations on production. Real gains for the worker come from what can be called the social uses of capital, one aspect of which is the dedication by industry of a large monetary investment in each worker. This fact is not understood or is overlooked by a good many people. I shall have more to say about the social use of capital in a later chapter devoted to the responsibilities of business to our society.

Remember that while American business has been enlarging its average investment per worker, it has reduced the tediousness and the length of the working day. A generation ago, workers in the steel industry had a twelve-hour day of great physical exertion at low wages; today steel workers have an eight-hour day with far less physical exertion required and several times the pay. During the past forty years, the average hourly wage of employees in the rubber industry has increased more than fourfold. Meanwhile the cost of tires has been reduced by half, and average tire life increased from thirty-five hundred to thirty thousand miles. Obviously employees, employers, and consumers have all benefited. And these are only two of hundreds of possible examples.

This is not yet the best of all possible worlds, and there are still challenges for improvement in every facet of the life of our own nation, but anyone who takes the time to draw up an objective credit-and-debit sheet for America's economic basis and goals will quickly be able to see how much is right with our conception and practice of free enterprise.

And capital remains, so to speak, the oxygen in the bloodstream of our economic system. To the man on the job, capital is far more important than any other element in the economy: it has provided him a fifty-ton shovel instead of a spade and wheelbarrow, thereby increasing enormously his productive power and thus providing him higher earning potential. As our population grows, we must invest an ever-growing amount in plant and equipment. Only in this way can the workers of tomorrow produce the goods and services necessary to defend and sustain a high and growing standard of living for an ever-enlarging number of people.

Every nation in the modern world is striving for increased capital formation to increase productivity, the Communist bloc included. Perhaps one of the reasons Communist leaders fight our free-enterprise structure so constantly is the fact that our way demands that more be given to the workers. The Communist societies are accumulating their capital by merciless manipulation of human lives in a totalitarian strait jacket.

The Soviets, particularly, are not concerned with profits or wages or fringe benefits for the labor force; freedom of the individual or of enterprise is not a requirement in their system. They have built military power and industrial strength in admittedly a phenomenally short period of time—but by limiting the individual worker practically to the barest necessities of life and appropriating a large share of the goods he produces for the strengthening of the state-controlled industrial machine. The fringe benefits for Soviet workers are slogans.

In contrast, we have built tremendous industrial strength—at a somewhat slower pace, but more effectively—while simultaneously giving our people the opportunity for a high and rising living standard. Our capital comes from the reinvestment of profits and the investment of the savings of millions of people—a method that requires much more initiative and imagination than does absolute government control. Our system, despite whatever shortcomings in practice it may still have, has resulted in the most fully productive economic system ever known; it has helped create twenty million more jobs than existed in 1940; it has allowed the worker's share of the personal income to increase from 78.4 per cent in 1929 to 89.7 per cent thirty years later; and it has given Americans a Gross National Product larger than five hundred billion dollars a year, the highest national income in the history of the world. That is indeed a record to be proud of and truly a system worth preserving.

THIS BRIEF EXAMINATION of the American economy has reviewed some of the basic facts of our free-enterprise system, much of what is right and healthy about it, and some of the factors that have made it strong. Now we should examine in general the subject of economic stability—what it is, how it is maintained, and what its trends have been in the history of our nation.

As we have seen, the long-time trend of American economic activity has been one of expansion. From decade to decade our productive capacity has increased; more people have been employed; individual worker income has risen; new and improved products have enriched our daily living. There have been, however, ebb and flood tides since the colonial period; during the intervening years our economic activity has moved in a reverse direction about one tenth of the time. We have gone through several major depressions, primarily those that began in 1837, 1873, 1893, and 1929, in comparison to which our most recent economic dips have been relatively mild recessions of short duration.

Some economic historians have pointed out that our economy has fluctuated fairly regularly, with the low point of the cycle coming every twenty to thirty years. None of these students has suggested that this is either desirable or unavoidable. Defense against extreme economic swings lies partly in insuring sound economic progress, partly in setting up adequate defenses against inflation before it begins. Our prime economic objective today, so far as stability is concerned, must be to keep a reasonable balance between the forces of inflation and deflation so that our total economy may have full opportunity for optimum growth and full employment can be maintained.

A healthy and stable economy is not one that stands still: it cannot; stability is the opposite of stagnation. Economic stability in workable terms means shorter business dips, with the total economic activity tending steadily forward—balanced growth without creeping inflation or falling prices—with general employment, increasing consumer demand, increasing production, and a bearable price level.

SINCE CONSUMER EXPENDITURE exercises the final veto on productivity and has also proved to be a highly stabilizing influence in our nation's economy, a great deal of the future course of the American economic scene will depend on the way the American woman uses her economic power. In the United States today, women control more than 60 per cent of personal expenditures. Mrs. America governs the spending of most of our annual national food bill of more than seventy-five billion dollars. By expressing her preferences in the market place, she sets standards of style and quality in many of our major industries. And in 1959 some four million housewives, the largest single group, owned stock in American industry, according to the New York Stock Exchange Census of Shareowners.

More than a century ago Alexis de Tocqueville, appraising the singular prosperity and growing strength of democracy in America, wrote: "It ought mainly be attributed to the superiority of their women." Tocqueville would be overwhelmed today.

Businessmen are generally a level-headed lot and most of them sensibly admit they do not understand women at all, but they do know something about the modern American woman's power as money manager. The statistics given above would by themselves make this clear; industrialists and economists admit, sometimes grudgingly, that the hand which holds the family bankbook rules our economy.

Many American women now also help earn some of the family income; about 38 per cent of married women in the United States have jobs outside their homes and contribute substantially to the total consumer buying power. There are now more than three million business and professional women, and economists who anticipate that our total national labor force will increase by ten million during the next decade have predicted that more than five million will be women.

Mrs. America can therefore be called a determining factor in our dynamic free-enterprise system. So long as she keeps her home standards high, demands the best in health services and education for her family, and provides her home with as much as she can afford of what progress can offer, the economic future of our nation is assured.

To HAVE PROGRESS we must have change. Business must perpetually adjust itself to consumer wants, an adjustment that brings ups and downs in various segments of the economy— "rolling adjustments" in which a rise in one segment tends to compensate for a decline in another. These adjustments usually appear among the three classes of consumer buying: in durables, semidurables, and consumer goods. For instance, a decrease in the demand for new houses (durables) may be counterbalanced by an increase in demand for automobiles (semidurables) or food and clothing (consumer goods).

These rolling adjustments can be so far-reaching, however, that they cause serious declines in several economic sectors at the same time. This kind of situation resulted in such recent recessions as those of 1948–49, 1953–54, 1957–58, and 1960–61. They were caused by a diversity of factors, but the result was that one or more areas of the economy went out of balance with the others and production exceeded demand.

No doubt some short-term economic adjustments will always result from the need to get output into balance with demand, and adjustments that result from innovation and improvement must be expected. When this happens it is necessary to curtail production until excess stocks have been worked off.

For stability, when it becomes necessary to cope with economic imbalance our chief concern should be to make the called-for adjustments in time to keep downward swings from deepening into serious depressions and upward swings into long periods of inflation. Such major swings are destructive and, in my opinion, avoidable. With the measuring sticks already developed, our economists should be able to detect developing imbalances and thus enable us to take preventive measures before major damage is done.

Students of economic phenomena have not been able to find a single cause for our "business cycles." Some explanations have actually attempted to connect business ups and downs to rainfall and agricultural-production cycles, which they in turn related to sunspots. Other explanations included failure of the monetary and banking system, declining prices, monetary deflation, rigidity in the price structure, overproduction, underconsumption, and national psychology. The amount of interrelation of these things as causative factors of economic instability is difficult to assess. The fact remains that we have had both times of inflation and periods of depression and that we must make every possible attempt to maintain a truly stable economy in the future.

The Great Depression of the 1930s illustrates particularly well how a modern recession can snowball into a depression and what happens when it does. This one started largely because the adjustments just after the first world war had started a boom that gathered momentum through the 1920s without a sound foundation of purchasing power. Prices declined through most of the decade. Employment, wages, and profits had begun to decline long before Black Friday 1929, but the stock market continued to climb. We raised our tariffs and stopped buying from abroad; this set the stage for a drastic decline in our export sales and resulted in a thoroughly unsound international trade balance.

Foreign indebtedness to the United States was increasing; our imposition of high tariffs at the same time made it almost impossible for debtor nations to repay us. Domestically, the rapid growth of more than one third in national income between 1922 and 1929 did not benefit large areas of the economy. As the agricultural boom stimulated by World War I came to an end, farm income was reduced. Wages were not keeping up with the growth in national income or gains in productivity, and the high-income groups were the principal beneficiaries of the false prosperity of the 1920s.

This situation resulted in greatly increased savings available for industrial investment—but most consumers did not have sufficient purchasing power to absorb the increased output these investments produced. In turn, this meant that only a small percentage of the funds available could be used for sound investment in plant facilities; the money left over created pressure for overseas investment as well as investment in trusts, holding companies, and all types of securities. Overspeculation was encouraged by too-easily available bank credit, dangerously low margins, and a relatively unpoliced stock market.

In October 1929 it became apparent that the stock market had reached a vulnerable position; a great many people tried to realize their paper profits or sell before prices fell further, and panic began. Stock prices plummeted. This was followed by further price declines in agricultural products and raw materials and reduction in international loans and trade almost to nothing. Production dropped by half. Businesses and banks failed. Unemployment rose to a full fourth of the labor force.

A portent that conditions in America had already begun to react on conditions in other parts of the world, these declines were not confined to the United States, and hope for an orderly recovery evaporated in 1931 with the collapse of the financial structures of pivotal European countries. Great Britain and at least a dozen other countries were forced off the gold standard. The resulting economic chaos intensified the situation in the United States. More and more banks failed, starting in the rural areas and spreading to the cities, and our own banking structure finally toppled in 1933. In all, about half of our banks had failed and perhaps one fourth of our total money supply was destroyed.

Government measures to improve conditions included various devices that were efforts to restore the financial system, raise agricultural purchasing power, increase exports, and encourage greater employment. The federal government insured bank deposits, launched construction of public works, endorsed loans to private business. Progress was slow; the final expedient was to use the power of the unbalanced federal budget to prime the country's economic pump. But unemployment still remained high: 9.5 million people were seeking work in 1939 compared to 12.5 million at the deepest point of the Depression in 1933.

The Great Depression lasted from 1929 until the beginning of World War II, recovery coming with the beginning of defense preparations for World War II. Gross national production did not regain its precrash 1929 level until the end of 1940. The government measures of the 1930s did not cure the Depression. They only helped to alleviate some individual distress through relief programs.

As a result of the Great Depression, much consideration has been given in many quarters to measures that can prevent a recurrence of such a calamity without putting our economy in the strait jacket of rigid economic controls. To accomplish this, one very important objective must continue to be the maintenance and enlargement of the purchasing power of the consumers of the nation. This is in fact currently being done partly by existing economic conditions, partly by a variety of social legislation, but most of all by an increasingly enlightened philosophy of management which seeks to have business constantly re-examine its operations to provide employment and create higher wages and increased purchasing power through improvement of the quality of its products and its methods of production, selling, and advertising. American industry has been making great advances, through research and technology, in increasing the productivity of mankind—the real source of gain in economic well-being—thus providing easier tasks and more leisure for its workers.

Perhaps the most powerful weapon at hand to fight incipient economic decline is that of tax reduction. This was not of much value before 1930, when federal taxes amounted to less than 4 per cent of the Gross National Product. With today's high tax rates—almost 26 per cent of our national income—if consumer-disposable income needs bolstering, a policy of tax reduction is available and effective.

Tax reduction for consumers can stimulate spending, thus eliminating excess capacity of industry and calling forth an expansion in business investment. A tax cut for business can make some projects more profitable while encouraging investment and healthy economic growth. A reduction in tax *rates* can therefore cause an offsetting increase in the tax *base* (incomes of both consumers and businesses) and tax *collections* can actually increase. This was precisely what happened following the

1954 federal tax cut. In less than two years federal revenues were higher than ever before—because the economy boomed.

Lowered taxation does not create permanent deficits in the economy to the same degree that enlarged government expenditures do. This is a fact that should be underlined in our thinking: reduced taxation can stimulate the economy and so enlarge the total national production that total revenues, even at lower tax rates, increase rather than diminish.

Another antirecession measure is present in the so-called automatic economic shock absorbers which help maintain consumer spending. These economic stabilizers include a consistent policy on the part of corporations to maintain employment and wages and often increase wage rates even in the face of declining sales and profits, stress on the importance of individual savings, social security and unemployment payments to individuals, the corporate profit tax (which absorbs slightly over half the decline in corporate earnings), and the personal income tax—which absorbs part of the decline in individual incomes. Consumer spending remains the most important of all our economic shock absorbers because it contributes so much to maintaining demand for consumer goods.

In each of our last four relatively small recessions (1948–49, 1953–54, 1957–58, and 1960–61), industry had to liquidate inventories to bring supplies of goods into line with falling demand. Such liquidations curtailed production, employment, and purchasing power temporarily, while lower earnings forced downward revisions of investment in plant and equipment. Personal incomes and consumption for the economy as a whole were nevertheless well maintained. Wage rates were actually increased, which helped offset the effect of shorter work weeks; employees who had to be furloughed received unemployment benefits; and old-age benefits continued without interruption.

Because consumers were able to maintain their expenditures

during the entire period that excess inventories were being reduced, production gradually began to increase again. Although business lowered investment in new plant facilities during these four postwar recessions, there was always shortly afterward a sharp rise in production in response to enlarged demand; sales requirements could not otherwise long be supplied. The production rise in turn further helped consumption and thereby reinforced recovery. The next turn of the wheel brought added investment in inventories and new facilities, enabling an upward cycle to begin once again.

It appears then that our economy is reasonably well equipped to fight recession and contain it, at least so long as it is not aggravated by adverse developments elsewhere. In any event, so long as consumers have adequate incomes, they will spend for what they need and want. If the demand for goods remains high enough, recessional adjustments cannot last long.

BUT WHAT ABOUT INFLATION? The traditional definition of inflation is "too much money chasing too few goods," a condition that results in a rapid increase in prices of such goods. In the twentieth century, especially after two world wars, the threat and the fact of inflation have been cruel problems for us. Genuine solutions to inflation hurt those who benefit from rising prices; inflation is an invisible tax that robs individuals on fixed incomes of part of their means of support or—if it goes high enough—of a major share of their subsistence.

The specter of inflation has not always been with us. In the century that preceded 1913, prices fell in more years than they rose. In fact, in 1939 the index of wholesale prices in the United States was lower than it had been in 1839. But from 1940 to 1960 the consumer price index rose from 60 to over 120! And today, in spite of efforts to control inflation, that index continues to crawl upward.

Inflation doesn't occur by chance; it has specific causes. Two powerful forces, for example, brought about the rapid price rise just before 1948. The first was enlargement of the money supply, the second the huge demand for goods created by World War II. In recent years a third force has been operative—wage increases in excess of the gains in average productivity per worker or per man-hour.

The enlargement of the money supply began in 1934, when the nation lowered its legally defined standard of gold content for the dollar from twenty-three to thirteen grains, so that each ounce of gold would make more dollars, and the value of an ounce of gold rose from $20.67 to $35. This step was taken initially to force prices up from their low 1934 levels. It did not work out, except for commodities in international trade.

It is the consumer who forces prices up, by spending more money—and in 1934 people did not have more money to spend. By law gold had to be turned in to the government at the pre-devaluation price; the only gain was to the federal government, which took for itself the profit when four billion dollars worth of monetary gold became seven billion. Business increased little; unemployment remained a major problem; and prices did not rise appreciably—only 5 per cent by 1940. But the stage was set.

When World War II engulfed the United States, our government desperately needed financial help. The banks responded by using their large reserves to purchase government securities. The federal treasury was thus loaned billions of dollars which it poured back into the economy as it financed the war effort and bought the goods and services it had to have. Money circulation leaped up. Bank deposits and currency soared from 71 billion dollars in 1940 to 176 billion by the end of 1945.

We had a greatly enlarged supply of money for spending without a commensurate increase in goods. Prices inevitably rose. In addition, the Federal Reserve System established a policy of giving market support to government securities by re-deeming them at par. This enabled banks to take their govern-ment securities to Federal Reserve banks and receive face-value credit. This in turn led to an immense compounding of credit. A single government bond could be sold to a bank for a thou-sand dollars—which the government spent. Then the bank could take the same bond to the Federal Reserve and receive another thousand dollars. This reserve credit could then be used by the bank to make more loans, which expanded bank deposits and the national money supply still more. Actually, inflation expan-sion occurs when banks create deposits by crediting the treas-ury's account for the government bonds they buy.

Trouble was in sight when this process continued at the time of the outbreak of the Korean War. Banks were rapidly expand-ing loans. Wholesale prices rose 15 per cent and the cost of living 10. We had allowed ourselves to be precipitated into more inflation.

In short, whenever we have too much money in circulation, we have laid the foundation for inflation. It is brought about when commercial banks have abundant reserves to supply an increased demand for ready money. As banks lend more, the supply of money increases. As more dollars become available, more people and corporations want to buy more goods—and prices rise.

THAT IS A BRIEF SKETCH of what inflation is. What about con-trolling it? The 1950–1960 decade provides a good example of how inflation can be controlled. When the Korean War broke out in June 1950, military expenditures increased greatly and prices rose sharply at both wholesale and consumer levels. This inflation was halted by a tax increase that produced a budget surplus the following year. Higher taxes reduced the purchasing power available to the public and enabled the federal government to pay for the Korean War without inflationary financing.

At the same time, supplementing heavier taxation, a tight-money policy effectively curbed bank expansion of credit. The tight-money policy was no more popular than the higher taxes, but while a few paid higher interest rates, this policy helped hold down prices for the majority.

As a result of these measures—and the controls in effect during the shooting war—the consumer price index, after its initial 10-per-cent rise, remained virtually steady for the five years from early 1952 through early 1956. Prices then resumed an upward trend, averaging about 2 per cent a year from 1956 through 1961. The inflationary effect of deficit financing was avoided by raising taxes, and the inflationary effect of undue credit expansion was held in check by tighter money.

HAVING LOOKED at the general proposition of inflation and its control, let us now consider the role of wage increases in a stable economy. There is no question that wage increases which exceed productivity increases raise unit costs, thereby forcing prices up and encouraging inflation—a factor called technically "cost-push" inflation. To avoid this kind of inflation, both labor leaders and business managers must make certain that wage increases for the labor force are balanced by greater production per man-hour.

Another cause of inflation is sometimes described as "demand-pull" inflation. When this occurs, prices rise because there is not enough additional product to supply the demand created by the additional dollars in the pay envelopes of the millions of employed people—a compelling argument against unsound wage increases, incidentally. This type of inflation has appeared particularly during and immediately following recent wars. High taxes and tight-money policies on the part of government have worked effectively to correct such excess demand in our recent history, as we have just seen. Most economists agree, however, that in the main the cause of price rises since World War II has been of the cost-push, not the demand-pull variety.

In the United States the average increase in the output per man-hour in nonfarm industry was 2.6 per cent annually from 1947 to 1956. But in the same ten-year period the increase in the hourly wage was substantially higher—5.5 per cent a year. The unavoidable result has been steadily rising unit labor cost and higher prices. During the same period, consumer prices rose an average of 2.2 per cent annually.

The wage agreements of 1959 and 1960 in the major industries did not actually cause immediate drastic price increases. The reasons for this were undoubtedly the large imports of steel in 1959 and the large flow of gold from the United States during 1959 and 1960. Such steel imports were clearly a warning that we were pricing ourselves out of competition (in this case, with foreign steel), and the considerable outrush of gold was a more general indication of the same warning. Of course, our balance of payments is also affected by American capital investments abroad, by our program of foreign aid, and by our military expenditures abroad. Gold is sold only to foreign official agencies which buy it either with accumulated dollars or dollars currently accruing to them. They have several reasons for wanting to buy gold from us with the dollars they receive (net) from their international transactions of all types, including their exports of goods and services to the United States.

The most obvious cure for our declining competitive position and our loss of gold is to hold down our prices. That requires holding down the causes of price increases—and since the main cause is excessive wage increases, public understanding and support for wise restraint and reasonable limitations on wage rises must be rallied. Many professional politicians have tended to ignore this root cause of price increases.

At the same time we must maintain a climate favorable to domestic investment. To make *invest in America* more than a slogan, attractive incentives and returns to capital must be assured within the country. This means a realistic, reasonable, and competitive tax policy and an equitable and sensible wage policy. We are competing with other nations for the investor's dollar as surely as for any other commodity.

THE UNITED STATES dollar has been considered for many years an unvarying measure of value, the soundness of which reflected the economic stability of our country. Since we own almost half of the world's gold, our currency has been considered completely dependable; after World War II the other leading nations of the free world anchored their currencies to the dollar, and we found ourselves the banker of the free world.

But many economic changes have taken place since World War II, especially since 1953. The productive structure of Western Europe and Japan has been rebuilt and made stronger than ever before. These countries are rapidly catching up to us in productive efficiency, and they are able to offer excellent goods on the world market at prices below ours because of their much lower wage structures. Our exports have been handicapped during the same period by the rising prices of our manufactured goods and our services—a rise that has been caused primarily, remember, by our constantly increasing wage scales, increases that are outdistancing our rise in productivity.

Today our economy again shows a deficit in our international balance of payments. Although our exports of goods and services continue to exceed our imports, our total money payment abroad is greater than our total receipts from abroad. Thus gold has been leaving the United States because of the sums we spend abroad on military and economic aid, on private capital investment by Americans in foreign lands, and on tourist expenditures.

Considering the international balance of payments of the United States for the years 1957–1960, only in 1957 did we have a net receipt of gold and dollars in the United States. That was the year of our immense increase in exports, partly because Western Europe, closed off from the Middle East by the Suez crisis, had to turn to the Western Hemisphere for oil and coal. In 1958 this boom was over; that year we suffered a payments deficit of 3.5 billion in gold and dollars, a figure that grew to 3.8 billion in 1959, due largely to an exceptional outflow of short-term capital at a time our trade balance was markedly improving. In 1960 our gold and dollar loss—or total deficit (imbalance) in payments—amounted to 3.8 billion dollars.

Because of this shift in trade and international payments, the outflow of gold from our shores has been to "settle the accounts." This outflow was intensified because many Americans and foreign investors are transferring funds to places in which interest rates and profits are higher than those paid here. And, in the fall of 1960, European speculators began to bid up the price of gold on the London free gold market because many of them assumed that the United States would eventually be forced to devalue the dollar by raising its gold price. Some think, quite wrongly, that this is our only solution to the problem of the gold and dollar drain.

Were the United States actually to depreciate its dollar, the move would wreak great havoc first on the large number of its citizens who are living on fixed incomes. Depending on Federal Reserve policy, such a procedure would expand the money supply from a given stock of gold and promote a further and substantial increase in the domestic price level. The competitive advantage that might thus be derived for our exports would be short-lived; the other nations of the free world would promptly take similar steps to place their exchanges once again in the earlier parity relationship with ours. The experiences of France,

Germany, Italy, and other nations have demonstrated the futility of exchange-rate depreciation and the destructive results of the monetary inflation that invariably follows.

Instead of the dangerous and unsound expedient of devaluing the dollar, what effective means *can* we employ to restore the balance between inflow and outflow of dollars? The easiest way —as well as the most rapid and the most intelligent way—would be to live within our means and to change the balance of all payments in our favor. Before we can do this, however, certain basic objectives will have to be attained.

To settle the balance—to correct the imbalance between dollar flow in and dollar flow out—our national budget will have to be kept in balance; in other words, we must see to it that inflation is checked in our own country. There must be no appreciable rise in our own price levels. Workers will have to forego unsound wage increases, however alluring they may be on the surface. We shall have to put much stress on increased productivity, which means among other things that inefficient "work rules" and "featherbedding" by both management and labor must be eliminated. Only if we can hold down unit labor costs can we control prices and compete with low-wage foreign production.

To assure a healthy trade balance, discrimination against our goods in tariffs and quotas by our allies will have to cease. Such discrimination, originally undertaken with our assent to enable them to replenish their dollar shortages, is no longer necessary. We must now be in a position to sell more goods abroad at competitive prices, and other nations must be willing to let them come in.

Also, restrictions by foreign governments against investment in the United States by their nationals must be eliminated. Our allies will also have to assume a much larger share of the burden of the joint defense of the free world; they must also contribute more economic aid to the less developed countries so that our burden in this area can be somewhat reduced. In addition, countries receiving foreign aid should be obliged to spend more of those dollars in the United States. In short, the solution is to extend more gifts of American-made goods and services, not of dollars or claims on our gold.

To summarize: To meet the challenge we face in the existing gold crisis and to get our international financial accounts into balance, several things are necessary. We must export more; we must persuade other industrialized countries to share more fully the moral obligation of aiding underdeveloped countries; we must ask other countries to eliminate their import restrictions on American goods, since we have lowered our tariffs; we must use more goods made in America for the support of our friends in the world's underdeveloped areas and for our military forces overseas; and we must insure a competitive and fair return on capital invested in America so that our dollars will remain at home and the world can have faith in the immediate and long-term strength and stability of the economy of the United States. Devaluation of the dollar would not do this; devaluation would only compound the problem and call forth damaging repercussions throughout the world.

Such are the general objectives that must be followed in the immediately called-for housecleaning that will put our financial house in order. We have at hand more than adequate means to accomplish these aims. But if we are going to come to grips with today's economic realities and keep our financial structure strong, the entire society must cooperate to that end—government, business, labor, and all our citizens. If we have such cooperation, there need be no concern in any quarter for the value of the dollar or the economic future of our country.

ONE OF THE HALLMARKS of a stable economy is growth, as I have already noted. And in the present time of change and challenge our own economic stability is closely linked with economic stability and growth in other countries. Whatever happens abroad echoes here, and vice versa. Foreign trade is essential to prosperity in practically every modern nation. By participating freely in such trade, we can assist other countries to develop and stabilize their economies. Simultaneously, we can use our own economic capacity more effectively. Lively foreign trade thus works in two ways to help promote our own welfare and the economic strength of other nations of the free world, in a way that no amount of well-intentioned unilateral effort on the part of the United States could accomplish.

In our domestic economy, for stability with growth we must always assure the maintenance of an adequate, stable, safe, and growing money supply. When the money supply contracts greatly, when business becomes bad and prices have no direction to go except down, there is a mad scramble for cash. The small independent bank cannot meet the demands on its funds. Bank failures of freezing of deposits have resulted in the deepest collapses in the economic history of our nation.

At the same time, it is also important to keep the domestic supply of money and credit from growing too fast or becoming too large. When money becomes too easy, excess funds seek an outlet in the excessive purchase of goods and investment. The available supply of goods cannot be enlarged quickly enough, so prices rise in an effort to balance supply and demand. The outcome is inflation, not sound economic growth.

AT TIMES it would almost seem in the discussion of our nation's economy and its stability today that the problem and the challenge boil down to the need to balance and counterbalance, to cooperate and expect cooperation on every hand. To a certain extent this is true, but there is nothing farfetched about it. Each segment of the society has a vital role in economic stability, today and for the future. The roles of government and of business are of particular importance.

The role of government is especially important because today government absorbs in taxes a full quarter of our total national income. Government must therefore formulate sound expenditure policies based on long-range realistic budgeting, correlated with equitable and growth-encouraging tax policies. Government needs to eliminate the inordinate waste brought on by unjustified crash programs that call for increased expenditures followed by reductions, adjustments, and delays in necessary projects.

In a related area, government needs to work unceasingly and courageously to find a real and lasting solution to the farm problem without undue further burden on taxpayers, thus bringing greater stability to the agricultural sector of our economy. It goes without saying that public works initiated by government play a considerable part in economic progress and stability; good highways, public building, and urban renewal programs, for example, are essential. Within limits, it is possible to accelerate the pace of public works when recession looms and to go more slowly in periods of rising economic activity.

Business, on its side, must also do its full part to maintain stability with progress. One of the causes of recession, as we have seen, is the liquidation of inventories of goods and a slowing of investment in plant and equipment. When the economy is on a down curve, the businessman reasons that it is better to wait before investing in new facilities. But when expansion resumes and he then has to add new plant, the price tag is higher. So the businessman has lost, both through the increased cost of plant and equipment and through delay in attaining more efficient production. Even more important, he has lost an opportunity to make his investment at a time when it would help take up some of the slack in the economy and thus assist in staving off government intervention of a type that is disadvantageous to free enterprise.

The vital point here is that industrial leaders must voluntarily accept the obligation to make every possible improvement in plant facilities in a sustained manner, regardless of momentary fluctuations in the economy. Some of our large corporations are already restating their faith in our way of life—and helping assure its continuation—by wisely planning their capital expenditures years in advance.

WHAT ABOUT FUTURE STABILITY? Our experience since World War II shows that we can have economic stability within reasonable limits *while* we expand economic activity to produce more goods for more people and raise the average standard of living. We have successfully contained four recessions within a narrow range, thanks to the automatic operation of built-in shock absorbers and the maintenance of consumer expenditures at a high level, and we were able to stop the inflation that followed the outbreak of war in Korea.

There is now every good prospect for a strong and growing American economy for at least the first half of the 1960s, and we can anticipate sizable future growth beyond 1965 as the needs of a coming population of four hundred million make themselves felt. And reliable current estimates predict that our Gross National Product will grow from its present 500-billion-dollar level to more than 750 billion dollars by 1970.

Future economic stability will require unselfish cooperation, wise planning, and realistic action on the part of business, labor, *and* government. It certainly behooves us, the strongest nation in the free world, to devote our vast collective talents to the achievement of the greatest possible stability for that economy.

We cannot permit ourselves ever to become complacent because the economic outlook is generally favorable. International competition is keen and growing keener—change indeed, and vigorous challenge. We must gear this uniquely workable system of ours accordingly if we are to serve well and to increase in stature, wisdom, and prosperity.

THREE

AMERICAN AGRICULTURE
AT HOME AND ABROAD

DURING THE PERIOD the thirteen American colonies were struggling for their independence and developing into a new nation, most of the civilized world still had basically an agricultural economy. Society was ripe for the almost unbelievable changes soon to be wrought by the industrial revolution—and, indeed, the influence of the growing local industries (small though they were by today's standards) in colonial America was one of the factors that helped speed the birth of our nation.

Nevertheless, the United States began as an agricultural nation, and such it long remained. Today we are an overwhelmingly industrialized and mechanized nation; even agriculture must be seen as an industry. But traditional ways of thinking and acting change slowly; many people talk about our "farm problem" today, and it remains a large political issue, but few enough people seem able to sift the facts and understand clearly the issues involved in agriculture's role in the United States in today's epoch of change and challenge.

One of the great advantages our country has had from the start has been its natural riches, high on the list of which is the fertility and variety of its soil. In fact, one of the facets of the farm problem today is an abundance: our surpluses of certain agricultural products. American citizens have been hungry and, a sad fact in the world's richest nation, some are still hungry.

But this is more a result of economic and political maladministration than of a basic poverty of available foodstuff.

Tragic hunger for many of the world's people has been a broad thread that has run through the recorded history of man, from Joseph's prophecy of seven fat years and seven lean years in biblical times to the twentieth-century fact so easy for Americans to overlook: that even today *three quarters of the world's people are undernourished.*

Even in the Western world until the nineteenth century, a state of hunger was accepted as the usual condition of most human beings. Just before the turn of that century Thomas Robert Malthus, an English clergyman-economist, pointed out that this would always be so and that world population would quickly begin to increase much faster than the available food supply unless held in check by war, pestilence, or famine.

Malthus was proved wrong, largely as the result of the agricultural and technological revolutions that took place after his lifetime. World population has expanded many times over—and so has its food supply. Here in the United States and in most Western nations there are no longer widespread food shortages. As I have already suggested, when some people go hungry or are improperly nourished in these countries it is not because of a lack of food. Here, poor distribution or poor diet—but plenty of money—may be among the causes. These countries tend to have food surpluses, not food shortages, and with them low prices for farm products and attendant problems for the farmers.

Since in the United States we do indeed have huge surpluses of certain foods, a number of people think that the shortages in other parts of the world could be remedied immediately by sending our surpluses where they are needed. The solution is unfortunately not so simple. Our agricultural surpluses are concentrated in a very few farm products—mainly wheat, corn, and cotton. Even if all the government-held surpluses of farm products in this country were distributed, great quantities of these products would not significantly alleviate food scarcity in other parts of the world.

EVEN IN THE relatively short period of our history as a nation, our agriculture has enjoyed periods of tremendous prosperity and has also suffered times of depression, crop failure, and famine. Over the long period, however, in the "agricultural revolution"—the application of scientific knowledge to the production of crops—remarkable advances have been made. Crop quality has been improved and yields increased. Today, American farmers are financially sound, as a group of the economy, probably sounder than ever before. In 1960, total U.S. farm assets reached a record high of 208 billion dollars and indebtedness was less than 12 per cent of assets—an enviable business record that shows remarkable solvency.

Ironically enough in view of the "farm problem," American agriculture has another record urban industry envies and wishes it could begin to equal. The incredible productivity rate of agriculture puts to shame the best efforts of business in our cities and towns. Between 1947 and 1956 the increase in productivity per worker averaged 6 per cent a year; during the same period nonfarm industries could not chalk up 3 per cent. Yet it is precisely this great accomplishment of the American farmer that has thrown him into a costly and difficult predicament—the present farm-surplus situation—in spite of his excellent average solvency.

The agricultural revolution began most fully to be felt when the motorized tractor replaced the horse and the mule as motive power and opened up ninety million additional acres for the production of food. Many other advances followed: new fertilizers used intensively, improved strains of plants and livestock, better methods of animal husbandry, and an almost staggering amount of efficient power machinery.

Farm tractors in use today can pull a three-ton cultivator across a field at a rate of nineteen acres an hour. One man operating such a tractor has many times the effective productive ability of his counterpart using the tractor available only twenty years ago. In 1830, using the reaper, forty hours of labor were required to harvest an acre of wheat. Today it takes one farmer and a self-propelled combine seven minutes.

THE PRIMARY RESULTS of such remarkable advances are a mixed blessing, and they are surely easy to identify: Many fewer people on farms are able to produce much larger crops than ever before. The population shift from farm to city continues as farms grow in size and are worked to a great extent with machinery. Surpluses appear quickly, farm prices fall, and the traditional American clamor for more government programs for farm aid grows louder.

So the first step in understanding (and therefore moving toward solving) the so-called farm problem is recognizing it for what it is—a social as well as a political and an economic matter. From the beginning politicians have set out to capture the farm vote. Some people have held that "old-fashioned farming," especially on the family farm, was a particularly beneficial way of life and should be preserved rather than apply technology and progressive methods to agriculture. Still others have announced that farmers have been denied their fair share of the national prosperity and that it is the duty of government to correct the inequity.

Such views at first have a superficial plausibility, but they are limited because they do not take into account what has actually been happening to American farmers and to the over-all

American economy in recent years; they neglect the fact that the major sectors of our society and its economy overlap and interact.

The continuing migration from farm to city involves both population movement in search of higher pay and the sale of farm land for the highest bid prices in our history. The movement also reflects the almost complete evolution of the United States from an agricultural to an urban-industrial economy. Even those who remain on the farms must expand and improve the efficiency of their operations.

The basic fact of farming today is that it has become an industry with modern capital equipment, and with many farms ranking as large and successful business enterprises. A good percentage of American farms are still family farms, but the number of small and therefore low-income farms is dwindling. In spite of all this, the somewhat romantic popular conception of agriculture still pictures it as a collective of small units facing insurmountable threats from wind and weather, and the general public tends to regard agriculture with the same sympathy it has for the small retail store trying to compete with the giant merchandising chain.

These sentiments leave out of consideration still another fact: much of the change in agriculture, during this century alone, is the result of strength and progress, not of weakness and despair. Our legislators have been quick to capitalize on such sympathies for vote-getting; the agricultural programs that have followed have been characterized by much faulty economics. Huge surpluses continue to rise—while the majority of the world continues to go hungry. Yet we cannot dispose of our surpluses without ruining world food prices and threatening the economies of many of our friends and allies among the nations that depend on the sale of agricultural products for their financial stability.

Facing the situation squarely and realistically, we must not only reduce our costly agricultural surpluses; we must also prevent their occurrence. Their continuing accumulation is now much more than a domestic problem; it is a formidable handicap in international relations. We quite naturally wish to be fair to our own producers of farm products, but in today's world we have a duty not to overlook the interests of our country as a whole and to consider as well the interests of other food-exporting countries, particularly our allies.

There is no easy solution to our farm problem. But our nation, confronted with either change or challenge, has never been afraid to evaluate the issues and do what needed to be done. It is high time for an objective, factual, nonpolitical re-examination of the "farm problem."

ON FIRST BLUSH it could seem strange that a businessman—an industrialist, if you will—has something to say about agriculture. Actually, it is not at all strange. The prime clue has already been given: agriculture today has become an industry much like our other, urban industries. This is a perfectly logical conclusion in view of the facts, but it appears one of the most difficult conclusions for many people to arrive at—especially politicians. Now that agriculture can produce so efficiently and abundantly for our needs, it should bear its own part of the heavy national burden and not automatically expect to be awarded the widespread public concern it enjoyed in the years immediately after World War II, when we had to feed starving people in Europe and elsewhere. Certainly in the 1960s we must appraise from a different viewpoint and without rose-colored glasses the farm industry now that we have more than nine billion dollars' worth of surplus food and fiber in storage.

There used to be a convenient cliché to the effect that economic depressions are farm-bred and farm-led. When our country was founded, nineteen out of twenty of its citizens lived on farms, and the volume of crops determined the movement of goods. If crops flourished, there was prosperity throughout as much of the country as was populated. Agriculture determined most of our exports and how many imports we could afford.

Today only one person in eleven in the United States lives on a farm; what happens to them affects the entire society but it can hardly any longer be said to be decisive in the economic fortunes of the urban population. A high level of business prosperity in our cities and towns, generating high wages and demand for farm products, coupled with the farmers' own consistent efficiency and productivity, is the real formula for agricultural prosperity. And prosperity in the city, with abundant job opportunities, is the best solution to the economic problem of the small displaced farmer.

During the past sixteen years more than twelve million people have moved from farm to city in the United States; during the same period our total national population increased by more than thirty million—with the highest birth rate in the rural areas. Urban industry has continued to offer farmers more and more jobs as the need for manpower in agriculture has declined, jobs that have afforded rising incomes. In this period, the sixteen years since the end of World War II, average weekly wages of all factory employees in this country have grown from forty-four dollars a week to more than ninety.

Just how well the adjustment to the great technological advance in agriculture has been made can be seen in the rise of per capita income for people living on farms. The welfare of a farmer or his family today is not measured by the number of bushels of wheat he raises or the number of acres he farms, or by the total income of all farmers. What is important is the total income divided by the number of people who must share it. In agriculture's three best recent years, 1947–1949, the per-person income of people living on farms averaged $851 annually. By 1958 this figure had risen above $1000 a year. Even though individual income figures for the urban population are higher than those for farmers, the rate of gain in per capita farm income has kept pace with the rate of increase for the people in cities. And, in many respects, the cost of living is lower and the non-monetary advantages are higher for the man who lives on a farm than for the city-dweller. Farmers may actually be better off today than many of them would admit, or even than some of them realize.

ANOTHER PREVALENT CLICHÉ in this area has been the observation that what is good for the farmer is good for America. This was widely true early in our history; it remains true today in the same sense that what is good for business or labor is good for the nation. The other side of this coin is frequently ignored, however: what is good for America is good for the farmer. We have now reached the state of our development at which the door has been left open to economic misfortune unless we keep in balance *all* the economic interests in our society.

Prices of farm products have long tended to fluctuate much more widely than those of manufactured products. This is the reason the Depression of the 1930s struck farmers so terribly and why a sweeping program of government assistance to agriculture was devised. The basis for the farm policies of the Depression years was sound. Agriculture needed instant help during a critical period. The government policy of buying commodities to support farm prices helped somewhat to raise the income of the farmer and his power to purchase the products of a depressed urban industry.

The price-support program was continued during and after the second world war. But during the 1941–1952 period, price supports were relatively ineffective; indeed, national policy sought to increase food production for the war effort, but the war-stimulated demand for food kept prices well above support levels. Fortunately, during this time the price-support program cost the government very little and few surpluses were accumulated—and the war-induced high demand also helped continue and increase the technological revolution in agriculture. Unfortunately, however, the continuing high support prices for agricultural products since 1952 have encouraged even greater production; farm surpluses have accumulated steadily and we now face a major national problem that increases each year.

Yet today, instead of relaxing supports in prosperous times and restricting government aid to a few critical farm commodities, price supports continue—largely to obtain votes. Congress continues to worship the sacred cow, to support the prices of certain farm products year in and year out. We somehow lack the courage and the perception to return to a free market for agriculture. We have doggedly pursued a course that has finally reduced agriculture to dependence upon government funds and government control. Some farmers apparently have the erroneous idea that through the referendum which enables them to vote on certain aspects of price supports and production or acreage controls, they have enough voice in their own planning and destiny.

They, and too many nonfarmers perhaps, continue to cling to outmoded concepts of what government should do for farmers. We still use money collected from the taxpayer to support prices and encourage farmers to produce more and more of what they cannot sell and what we as consumers do not want. We should use this money to help farmers produce the things we do want, the things they can sell.

THE PRIME DIFFICULTY with rigid price supports at high levels is the fact that they prevent prices from performing their normal and useful function of guiding production and consumption. Prices in a free market are the link between the producer and the consumer. This relationship is thrown out of effective balance when the government stands ready to buy—at a fixed price which encourages a larger output by the producer—any products the consumer does not want at this same price.

High price supports for certain commodities encourage farmers (because it is profitable) to raise too much of these commodities. Wheat is an example. There have been temporary periods of overproduction of other products, such as potatoes and eggs, but these problems were promptly corrected when the dynamics of the market place were free to operate—when, that is, prices were freely flexible.

It should be plain that price supports for agriculture—or for any other industry—which are out of line with domestic and international conditions are economic foolishness and that the consequences in the long run will be serious. The bait is honey-sweet to the producer, temporarily. It will not be long, however, before other pressure groups begin to demand government protection and underwriting of their special interests. Controls beget controls; as a taxpayer the initially supported producer finds himself paying for the gain of some other interest.

Production is the only path to abundance in our world of endless need and desire. But production that is not used to satisfy want, that merely adds to surplus, is disastrous waste of scarce and valuable resources.

WE THEREFORE REMAIN faced with the present farm crisis in the United States. The federal government has had great success in solving a number of farm production problems through research and education, but it has not been able to solve the problem of markets and surpluses. The primary reason is legislative misdirection. It is perfectly fair to say that the surplus problem has not developed because of weaknesses in *administering* the price-support program. It is mainly the result of the legislation that instituted and perpetuated the policies and the high levels of support prices, which offer considerable incentive for the farmer to overproduce.

I have already shown that the cost of this folly is huge, simply by noting that at the end of 1960 the government had about nine billion dollars' worth of surplus farm products stored in granaries and warehouses across the land. The farm program as a whole continues to cost the taxpayer more than five *billion* dollars a year. The cost merely to store and handle present surplus products is nearly three and a half million dollars each day.

In 1960 we had a wheat surplus of more than a billion bushels —an amount sufficient to supply all domestic and export markets and leave a normal carryover into the next year even if no more wheat at all were produced for a year.

Our huge surpluses of agricultural products are not competitive and therefore are not easily salable in the international market: our prices are too high for the "have-not" countries. We have indeed exported large quantities of wheat and wheat flour under the surplus-disposal program made into law in 1954, Public Law 480. But the amounts marketed under this legislation have not been adequate and we have often been obliged to take payment in local currencies rather than in dollars. We have therefore not solved the surplus problem; we have only prepared the ground for new problems.

FURTHER TO COMPOUND THE PICTURE, the present price-support program gives the least help to those who need it most, the farmers with the lowest incomes. About one third of our farms produce only 2 per cent of all farm products. Price supports help these farmers very little because they have so little to sell in the market place. For the most part, these are people who have small acreages and carry on modest farming operations; as a group they have off-farm jobs which bring them nearly seven billion dollars a year in wages.

The principal beneficiaries of high price supports are quite a different group: the big farmers who have a great deal to sell. The present support program benefits the 47 per cent of our farms which account for 90 per cent of total farm production. Most of the government checks—and the largest—go to the big farmers with greater productivity and larger earning power, and who need help the least.

This is not the only upside-down aspect of our support programs for agriculture. Price supports apply mainly to wheat, cotton, corn, rice, peanuts, and tobacco—crops for which American consumers do not either want or need expanded output. Yet these supports continue to encourage production precisely where we do not want more production and where usually we want less. For livestock, for which there is increasing demand and which makes up about half of farm production, there is almost no farm price-support assistance.

BEFORE WE LOOK at possible solutions and the subject of putting our existing farm surpluses to work, let us summarize the chief points of today's farm-problem situation.

Our present farm policies promote surpluses, reduce farm income, weaken the farmer's independence in the long run, and make him dependent upon a government which can decree how much he shall get for his product and how much of it he may produce. Guaranteed price levels and acreage controls have not decreased surpluses or the difficulties attendant upon them. Inflation is encouraged; government planning and bureaucracy increase. These are all direct consequences of our futile attempts to flaunt the economic laws of supply and demand.

The "farm problem" is actually a number of problems in which there are two main categories: (1) surpluses and what can be done about them; (2) maintenance of farm income at an economically reasonable level.

The problem of surpluses also subdivides into two parts. The first is what we can do to prevent further accumulations. The second is the challenge to find ways and means to use present surpluses usefully. Genuine solutions are not likely to be easy or politically popular.

There can be no argument about the farmer's right to an equitable share of our growing national prosperity—provided that he in turn is willing to recognize the economic facts of life and to synchronize his efforts with the needs of our society and those of the rest of the world. The job may be a difficult one, but the farmer must try.

Farmers cannot expand or contract their output of various products as easily and quickly as an urban manufacturer can. Having charted his course, the farmer must carry it through until his crops mature and his animals are ready for market. For that reason, and because food and fiber are so essential to our society, the farmer is entitled to know that society is willing to accord him special consideration in guarding him from major catastrophes in the discharge of his service to it.

A peacetime farm program should therefore include some kind of income insurance for the farmer. Under such a scheme the government would provide compensation for farmers when their incomes fall below some realistic, predetermined level. Whatever changes in policies are made, the small-acreage and low-income farmer must be given special consideration and assistance.

IN FACING SQUARELY up to the problems of American agriculture today, we should now consider action along seven main lines:

1. We must vigorously expand our programs of research to find new markets and new uses for our farm products both at home and abroad. More study must be given to the effects of population growth, trends in food-consumption habits, the effects of improving technology, and possible industrial uses for agricultural products. We must try to get a fairly clear picture of our future food and fiber needs, the sources that can supply them, and how much land and resources these needs will require. If we can see in perspective both our own needs and what we may reasonably expect to export, we can compare the findings with our present production and make the necessary adjustments. Government can then help people on marginal and low-income farms to find ways to make a better living. The finding of new markets and new uses for farm products, of course, will not produce quick results.

2. We must take additional steps to increase our "Food for Peace" program to meet the needs of less fortunate people in the world.

3. We must continue to negotiate for and work toward free international trade. Our prices must be reduced sufficiently to provide markets for our surpluses abroad at prices consumers there can afford to pay. We must purchase more from nations abroad so they may obtain the dollars necessary to buy from us, while at the same time we leave no stone unturned to promote the sale of our own products abroad.

4. We must make honest public disclosures of the costs of farm subsidies and of the issues involved. More objective and more complete information concerning farmers' incomes and living standards must become available. We must find out who the "poor" in agriculture actually are and how they can best be helped.

5. We must expand the Conservation Reserve Program of the Soil Bank. Much more land must be conserved and its fer-

tility restored. The land that is being worn out growing surpluses today may well be desperately needed tomorrow to support the population explosion.

6. We must adopt policies to promote full employment and general prosperity through the national economy. A prosperous and growing urban economy means jobs at high wages for displaced farmers and abundant markets for farm products.

7. We must give enthusiastic support to the Rural Development Program which has as its objective the improvement of living standards of small, low-income farmers through local, state, and federal cooperation. In this program, already under way in more than thirty states and in Puerto Rico, government agencies assist rural and urban citizens in developing the resources of the local community.

Action along all or even several of these lines can bring the beginning of a real solution to our farm problem.

The farmer should not be exposed to the forces of the market without some protection, but such protection must not be allowed to become either an incentive to overproduce or the basis for overpricing. We must make certain that no farm policy impairs the functioning of the free market.

If we eliminate the free market, or if we allow it to be subtly undermined, we throw the issue into politics and step onto the road away from freedom toward total government—a road none of us in labor, agriculture, or business wants to travel. When we strengthen the free market as the governor of the economic well-being of people, however, we strike a blow for individual freedom and progress throughout the entire world.

FOOD SURPLUSES—and it is abundantly clear that our country has them—are not altogether bad. A stockpile of food products for national defense and for the assistance of hungry human beings at home and abroad can be useful. There is nevertheless an important difference between a reasonable inventory of food which can be helpful in our domestic welfare programs, national defense, and foreign policy and, on the other hand, unreasonable and growing surpluses that are the result of unwise agricultural policy dictated by political expediency.

We cannot afford the luxury of unused and useless surpluses so long as we are engaged in a life-and-death struggle with communism. Today we are an island of plenty in a world of want and starvation—a world in which we must strive for the friendship of almost two billion people who exist without adequate food and shelter, to say nothing of lacking even the most trivial creature comforts we take for granted.

And also consider the almost unbelievable population expansion that is continuing. World population today numbers just under three billion people. By 1975 there will be more than four billion, if the present growth rate continues. And by far the largest increase will come in the underdeveloped nations of the world, those with the fewest resources and the smallest food supplies.

Here lies the greatest challenge to our way of life. The continuing population explosion and its concentration in the underdeveloped areas exercises a grave and increasing threat to the security of the entire free world. The Communists know that more than half the world's people live in countries that are still "uncommitted" either to the East or to the West. They realize that if they can win over these underprivileged peoples they can overthrow freedom and gain the world for themselves far more easily than by waiting and infiltrating economically healthy societies.

And the Communists know they can often win over individuals and nations by the simple expedient of assuring that they are furnished enough food to eat.

Some day—and I pray that day will come quickly—it will become politically popular in the United States to reshape our farm policies to meet this challenge and to use our great productive power to win friends for freedom by satisfying some of the overwhelming needs of the rest of the world. I do not have the slightest doubt that the imbalance between farm income and other income as well as the problem of agricultural surpluses can be satisfactorily resolved if we take bold and courageous action. If we will search objectively for the best solutions and if we will refuse to yield to the pressures of special interests, the farm problem will be solved and the economic well-being of people will improve both at home and abroad. And freedom will gain.

Agriculture is a rich mortar that can hold together the stones in our foreign policy—or it can be a primary cause of our loss of the Cold War. Our foreign policy today is going to influence the future of every person in the United States for generations to come. American agriculture has a positive role to contribute to these foreign affairs.

The world need for food is great. If America does not re-examine its farm problem in the context of world problems (as well as in terms of acres and government programs) it could be signing an invitation to eventual defeat.

FOUR

GOVERNMENT AND BUSINESS

ONE OF THE exciting things about America is the way in which all segments of the society can (and, indeed, must) interact and contribute to the full life of the nation. This voluntary and spontaneous assumption of responsibility by the parts for progress of the whole is a fundamental basis for our greatness as a nation. In our general economy, as in our governmental structure, there are healthy and desirable checks and balances. This tends to make life somewhat complicated, much more so than if we were the strait-jacketed inhabitants of a totalitarian state.

Our nation has prospered because it has continued to be a free society. We have never had—nor do we wish—one single architect of progress. All of us occupy the position of equals, whether our chief endeavors are in government, in agriculture, labor, business, education, or one of the professions. Freedom as we conceive it does not allow one area to usurp either the prerogatives or the responsibilities of the others.

This system also allows us to take a healthy and critical look both at the sector of economic life in which we work and at what is going on in the others. But neither our free system nor our challenging times allow us to take lazy refuge in political stereotypes or unthinking characterizations of other segments of our national life.

Take the interaction of government and business, for example. It is much easier to take a superficial view and characterize our side as the "good guys" and the other one as the "bad guys" than

73

it is to get down to issues and define the responsibilities of each. To keep the machinery of our free society in best working order, however, such definition is what we must have.

Government is the agent of the people for the whole public interest; it is "We, the people." Business is that aspect of our society organized to produce and distribute goods and services. Business cannot attempt to play the role of government, and government was not set up to run the affairs of business.

IN OUR FREE SYSTEM, government's basic economic function is the promotion and mediation of the over-all best interests of all productive elements in our society—farmers, laborers, management, owners of enterprises, and most important, consumers. Government should always ask what is best for the consumer— and since we are all consumers, that means the general public.

Just as business learned long ago it must constantly re-examine its operation, our federal government today can very properly take a look at its own household. It already has a wise blueprint for more efficient modern operation in the two reports of the Hoover Commission. Some of the Commission's recommendations have in fact already been put into practice and many tax dollars already saved thereby. Greater efficiency, making it possible for government to function at lower cost, is indeed worth pursuing. Perhaps the amounts which can be saved are small in relation to the size of the federal budget. But whatever the amounts, they are indefensible wastes. We need continuing research and re-examination for efficiency in government. And we need more courage on the part of government itself to put these recommendations to work.

What our society needs most from government is efficient and positive action that will nourish our free economy and speed up the flow of savings into invested capital and productive power: this is the way our economy grows. Sane and reasoned government policies can create an atmosphere favorable to free and competitive enterprise—not for the sake of American business alone, but also as a powerful stimulant to economic growth for the welfare both of the American people and of the rest of the free world. Government must assure that no controls are imposed on business in such a manner as to restrict or cripple the economic power of the United States. In short, government has an overriding obligation to all society to clear away obstacles that block the flow of investment and discourage the development of new methods of production, new products, and better services.

BUSINESS' FUNCTION is to promote the general welfare by producing the thousands of things in millions of styles and sizes and colors our citizens of all ages need and want in their daily living. According to our American way of thinking, government does not tell us what we must buy or how we shall spend our money. Freedom means that individuals, not the government, shall decide what they want and how much they are willing to pay for it.

There has to be a system of free markets where consumers can exercise freedom of choice before their needs and desires can guide and direct the producer of goods. The individual consumer tells the producer through the distributor and retailer what goods he wants and what prices he will pay for those goods. That message flows through free markets. The producer responds by supplying more of the goods the consumer wants and will buy and by curtailing production of the goods the consumer has indicated he will not buy.

The free-market method of communication from consumer to producer is totally disrupted when an agency so powerful as government steps in to fix prices and buy products the consumer does not want at these prices and which the government cannot sell at the higher prices it paid for them. Today some of our national policies result in exactly this kind of upside-down government interference in our free-market system. Our price support policies in agriculture, for example, require the government to buy farm products to sustain prices higher than consumers want to pay. These are precisely the things consumers want less of, yet farmers are encouraged to produce more of the products. The result is that farm surpluses pile up—surpluses which nobody wants at these high prices. Unfortunately, the American taxpayer seldom stops to realize that it is he who pays for such foolishness. The burden of losses incurred by the government from the purchase of farm surpluses will be borne by the individual consumer in higher taxes and higher prices than he wishes to pay for the food products he needs.

FREEDOM FROM "big government" is an honored American tradition, but sometimes we are a bit muddle-headed about precisely what this has meant in the nation's history. We readily say that in a free country such as the United States, government should not interfere with our private lives. We begin to get hot under the collar about new controls government may place on us, and we shout that each change violates the American Way.

But government has been regulating our lives in one way or another: we have long had taxes and tariffs, the draft and selective service, and government control of the postal system, waterways, and highways. Now in addition there is government regulation of air traffic, radio and television channels, and there is much more under the heading of interstate commerce.

Even with the wisest and most conservative available leadership in these times, we are bound to have more bureaucratic interference with all our activities than the Founding Fathers could possibly have forseen. In George Washington's time, the job of government was much less complex than it is today. When nearly every family lived on a farm and produced its own food, clothing, and many of the other things it needed, there was relatively little work for government.

Today our economy is exceedingly specialized, enormously complex and highly interdependent. We have moved from a horse-and-carriage to a jet-plane and potential space-ship age. Coordination of all our diverse activities has become an ever-growing problem, a problem that can be met only by all of us together—by "Us, the government." Necessary government controls within rational limits must referee the constant operational and human stresses among the men who own the money and risk buying the machines, the men who work the machines, and the people who buy the products the machines and men turn out. But today American industry quite rightly fears the ever-growing controls government is imposing on our economic life. Indeed, many of these controls are hindering progress and occasioning a loss of welfare, not alone to private business but to the whole of society as well.

American taxpayers—all of us—are supporting expenditures that exceed forty billion dollars a year for military defense, some 10 per cent of the Gross National Product. Experts estimate that nearly a third of the United States' economic activity (including a host of dependent enterprises civilian in name only) are either based on or the companies involved derive most of their sales from the present international armaments race. Whether or not this is good for the free-enterprise system, it does call attention to the increased interrelation that now exists between government and business and hints the danger that the arms race could force even our country toward a military socialism if it is not managed wisely and carefully.

Even the most rock-ribbed industrialist in the United States will agree that certain controls are necessary for the general good. The Federal Trade Commission, the Federal Reserve Board, the Securities and Exchange Commission, and the Food and Drug Administration have been effective in protecting the best interests of all the people to an extent they certainly could not do for themselves, as have controls in the fields of aeronautics and communications, which are now required to minimize accidents and transmission confusion. These are matters, all agree, that cannot be handled adequately either by individuals or by the individual states. These controls validly belong to the federal government.

We therefore need regulation in such fields, but always with caution. There is a clear and ever-present danger in the increasing tendency in some government circles to interfere with free-market operations and to make economic decisions on the basis of political expediency rather than what is truly best for our country. Once demagogy takes the place of democracy, once political power takes the place of the rational free market, we are hopelessly on the road to the totalitarian state.

Every time we allow another unnecessary control on American business we weaken freedom for all of us, including those outside business. Every time we block an unnecessary control we cast our lot on the side of individual freedom, economic progress, and human betterment.

THERE IS ALSO the question of social welfare, one in which both business and government are concerned today. I have indicated some of the important social responsibilities of business in a later chapter. So far as government is concerned (as in our time it is concerned most deeply) with matters of social welfare, there are at least two factors that must be borne in mind. The first is the insidious tendency of the members of a society to want government to do for them more and more of the things they should and could do for themselves, the desire for a fairy-godmother state.

The second factor is expense. Government agencies designed

to confer social benefits on the nation all cost money. As I am using it here, *money* is another word for the taxes that must come from every level of our society. It is the responsibility of business and government, indeed the responsibility of all Americans, to make certain that social-welfare expenditures are not so enlarged that they dry up the feeder streams of progress in our economy. We must take care that the burden placed on the productive does not destroy their productiveness.

Investment capital comes from business earnings and from the saving of personal income. Excessive diversions from our capital structure would in time undermine production, and excessive taxes on capital sources must be avoided if we are to continue to expand our industrial plant. We must not allow government to promise so much security and provide so many de luxe services that we undermine the incentive system which has produced excellence in our people and greatness in our country. If we do, economic stagnation and regimented living will be the terrible price.

We must have a yardstick against which to measure the ultimate value of new social-welfare schemes before taxpayers are saddled with the cost of such additions. This could consist of two questions: First, does the added cost of the new welfare program interfere with the capital needs of a vigorous economy, the ultimate source of real abundance? Second, will the added costs cripple the forces of incentive competition and free enterprise which are so essential if we are to expand our flow of goods and services and maintain our national strength? If the answer to one or both of these questions is yes, then the disadvantages of such a move far outweigh the benefits to our society.

Nor can the cost of welfare measures be allowed to become such a burden that it breaks the back of the enterprise system that feeds and clothes and houses our people; welfare costs must not take so much from our capital structure that they jeopardize our productive power. Welfare costs must not take so much from the worker in society that he loses his willingness to strive and produce excellence. There is a point beyond which we cannot safely go and still leave sufficient incentive and stimulus to do our best and to get things accomplished.

On the other hand, free enterprise should not always register blind resistance to every social-welfare measure government proposes. A truly democratic society cannot be run solely to the tune of the needs of business corporations or labor unions or of any other special-interest group. The first duty of government is the guarantee that the society is maintained for the benefit of all the individuals in it.

This is particularly applicable to "public assistance," that special area of social welfare in which the government assumes responsibility for helping needy citizens and the aged who do not have enough to meet the essentials of living. The cost is borne by state and local governments with the help of federal grants-in-aid.

Public assistance is necessary even in periods of prosperity and full employment; there are always some people in need as a result of such conditions beyond their control as old age, illness, or disability. Public assistance has a specific and valid purpose to serve in our general social-security system, but it is not (nor should it ever be allowed to become) a substitute for work and individual responsibility.

For example, in our country there exist so-called seriously distressed areas in which the general need is so extensive and the standard of living so low that local public-assistance programs cannot possibly do a satisfactory job. Perhaps for people in these areas, and others in our society where the requirement is equally valid, we should re-examine and improve our other social-security programs. But since the most effective of all measures to help the needy is to offer them an opportunity to earn a good living, the first line of attack by government should be the development of measures to promote full employment in these distressed areas as well as throughout the economy.

If these broader and more effective steps to help the needy are taken by promoting a prosperous and growing economy, social-welfare and public-assistance programs of all kinds can assume their proper and limited role. Public assistance can then become a flexible program, to be expanded or contracted as economic conditions require. Thus the truly needy people who are not able to call on other services can still obtain the assistance necessary to maintain a minimum standard of living.

The major recent criticisms of public assistance have been that it is too expensive, that we have too much of it in prosperous periods, that it destroys initiative and fosters dependency, and that it destroys pride and humbles the individual who must seek it—criticisms that to a large extent are not valid.

So far as expense is concerned, the fact is that there is a great deal of need still not being met. The costs of public assistance could be decreased if there were more and better programs to promote full employment. Public assistance does not promote need merely because it helps alleviate it any more than it promotes illegitimacy because it makes available assistance to children born out of wedlock.

The average beneficiary of public assistance wants to get off the relief rolls as soon as possible; it is the exceptions who make the headlines and provoke most of the attacks on such aid. Our people do not like asking for help. There are widespread proofs that Americans want work, not relief; that they want independence and dignity, not pampering by government dole. This is exactly as it should be.

We are now spending more than three billion dollars a year on public assistance—money that provides food, shelter, and clothing for more than six million of our citizens. We do not yet have reliable data on whether this promotes dependency or whether it helps people regain the road to independence. The outspoken critics would accomplish much more about this issue if they would seek accurate answers rather than expend energy in debating the matter.

We do need more data than are now available. We need more exploration, research, studies, and demonstrations in connection with effectiveness of the public-assistance and all other social-welfare programs. We need reliable information on such matters as the attitude of the community toward recipients of public assistance and the effect on individuals of adequate or inadequate assistance. We also need studies to determine whether or not aid programs weaken or strengthen family life. Both business and government have a stake in this matter.

AND BOTH BUSINESS and government have an equal stake and duty in maintaining the America we know, believe in, and want to keep strong. So do labor, agriculture, and the professions. The most important fact that must emerge from any discussion of business and government is that they are here to stay—in our system of life—and that by meeting fully the responsibilities that are properly theirs they can keep that system alive.

Excellence, whether in government or in industry or anywhere else, is not something one arrives at. It is something one continues to strive toward. Constant research, re-examination, and correction is a necessary part of the process. And this is definitely true of all our programs for social welfare. We must work efficiently to help people—to help themselves.

FIVE

TAXATION AND TAX REFORM

IN A SUPREME COURT DECISION, Justice Oliver Wendell Holmes observed crisply, "Taxes are what we pay for civilized society." One of the prime early forces of the struggle for independence that led to the establishment of the United States was unjust taxation, and the rallying cry became "No taxation without representation."

In more modern times, taxation tends to be felt personally and intensely. With the approach of the middle of April every year in the United States, popular comedians and magazine cartoonists capitalize on the situation of John Q. Citizen trying to prepare his own tax return—and on his frustration at the complexity of the tax form, the approach of the deadline, and his irritation that he has to shell out to pay "the government."

Even Benjamin Franklin, writing in a private letter in 1789, reported that "Our Constitution is in actual operation; everything appears to promise that it will last," then appended half-solemnly "but in this world nothing is certain but death and taxes." Franklin would readily have admitted, however, that intelligent and necessary taxation helps pay the cost of freedom.

That cost has risen since Franklin's time. So has the national standard of living. In fact, today's semiskilled laborer lives in conditions of comfort that in many aspects would have been beyond the imagination of the wealthy and privileged in the first years after the War for American Independence.

Taxes, like the weather, are considered by a great many people a matter everybody talks about and nobody does anything about—the implication being that nobody can either understand them or do anything to change them. In our country, in the case of taxes if not of weather, if enough people do understand the structure and collectively believe that something is wrong with it, something *can* be done to adjust the situation. Taxation in a free society in the modern world is indeed inevitable, but—unlike death or even the climate—something can be done about them.

Therefore let us take a look at taxation in America today. We may raise more questions than we have immediate answers for, but these are points worth examining, always bearing in mind that sensible taxation is the price of our chosen kind of freedom.

To THOUGHTFUL AMERICANS in the middle of the twentieth century, one of the most disturbing developments in the domestic economy is the rapidly growing cost of government. In the view of many this cost, which finances services that range from a strong defense through health, education, and welfare to the maintenance of national parks and interstate highways, has become a distinct threat to individual incentive to work and save and to our ability to produce and to keep our economy progressing. Surely it is obvious that the more and bigger the services we demand of government, the more it will cost us in taxes.

Major taxes in the United States today fall on the incomes of individuals and corporations, estates and inheritances, property, and the myriad of goods and services we buy. Our most important tax problem is to have tax systems at all levels of government that balance one another and are designed so that they promote business enterprise and permit our free-enterprise system to flourish. However, the overlapping and almost competitive race by federal, state, and local governments to exploit every possible revenue source makes the problem complicated and difficult. Both the foundation of our country's economy and the chief source of tax revenue for government at all levels is the private-enterprise system. When the tax burden becomes so great as to interfere with the best economic performance of individuals and businesses who make up our private enterprise system—as some believe it now has—we are faced with a fearsome dilemma because the tax base contracts and government cannot find sufficient tax revenues for its needs.

Take the income tax, for example. The amount of income tax revenue actually collected by the government depends on the tax rate and the size of our income (tax base). Now, if the tax rate is raised so high as to discourage production and destroy jobs and incomes, the amount actually collected by the government will fall. Federal, state, and local governments therefore have big stakes in our individual and corporate earnings and in the perpetuation of a prosperous and growing private economy. It would be well to warn those in government circles who would wield the tax axe not to kill the goose that lays the golden eggs. In fact the important thing is to improve the health of the goose. Today taxes are high. The economy is producing less than it should by almost fifty billion dollars. The tax rate is thus too high. It is repressive. Lowering the tax rate could expand the economy—make the goose so healthy that more eggs would be laid for everybody, including the government.

In 1960, taxgatherers at all levels of government collected more than one quarter of our country's Gross National Product —some 137 billion dollars. The question that begins to emerge is what will happen when this amount, paid in taxes, is in effect diverted from the productive channels of our economy. With a reasonable flow of these tax dollars to government there can be no justifiable quarrel. Indeed, some government taxes and expenditures, such as those for education and research, are an aid to private enterprise and add to the mainstream of our economy.

But excessive taxes can have serious results, and basically unwise tax policies over the long haul will prevent economic growth.

The compelling issue therefore begins to be the need for our collective decision whether we want to call upon and rely upon the government to do more things for us than it has been doing, or whether we wish to do things for ourselves through a truly free and vigorous system of private enterprise. Happily, a great many Americans believe that the best way to provide the highest standard of living for the most people is through free enterprise, not big government and ultimately socialism. Instinctively, as well as after careful consideration, most of us realize that we want and need a tax system so organized that freedom and private enterprise will flourish.

In 1950 (before the Korean outbreak) and again in 1955, tax reduction in the preceding year was followed by a very large increase in total tax revenues. At the same time, because we had high production and high employment and therefore enlarged tax revenues, increased federal spending was very small relative to tax gain. As we succeed in maintaining a high employment economy, we reduce the need for government benefits and spending.

For example, in fiscal 1956 federal budget receipts rose by 7.6 billion dollars; federal expenditures, in contrast, increased only 2.8 billion dollars. That was a period of marked economic growth and increased productivity. As a result, revenues increased almost three times as much as expenditures. A still more striking period is reflected in the results for fiscal year 1960. Budget receipts in the economic recovery of 1959 were enlarged in the budget for fiscal 1960 by almost ten billion dollars, whereas expenditures actually declined by more than three billion. The decline in expenditures was the result of having "put through" a number of nonrecurring expenditures in the previous year's budget so that budget outlays actually fell in fiscal 1960.

The first clear question, then, when we think about the best tax program for our country, is: How large a portion of our national production can we turn over to government and still keep our economy strong? Perhaps we are approaching the limit of taxes compatible with a vigorous and growing economy. I hope we have not indeed passed this limit already.

ALMOST AS LONG AS human history has been recorded, pleas to reduce taxes have been heard. The last reduction in U.S. federal income tax rates, which came in 1954, still left both individual and corporation rates higher than they had been before the Korean War. Ever since World War II state and local taxes have been rising steadily. In the same period the combined debt of all levels of government—federal, state, and local—has increased greatly.

In the long run, we must balance the budget on all levels of government—expenditures must equal tax collections. What that means is if taxes are to be lowered, government expenditures must be cut or the base enlarged. The principal factor which would permit a lowering of taxes would be a halting or at least a slowing down of the mounting trend toward more and more de luxe government services. Most people today agree that we should eliminate waste and by operating efficiencies reduce the cost of providing government services, but from a practical point of view, little if any tax reduction can be expected here. It is a fact of economic life that the scope of government programs we choose is what will determine whether or not we can have any tax relief.

Economic growth offers another way of reducing our tax burden. If we expand our national production and incomes, the mounting unavoidable and desirable costs of government will be more easily bearable. Growth in the private sector of the economy can be expedited in three ways: (1) We should continue to invest billions of dollars to improve our factories for the purpose of increasing the productivity of our workers and to make our products competitive in world markets. (2) We should expand research for the development of new products and better methods of production. (3) We should cultivate more intensely and broaden the markets for our economy's products at home and abroad. This kind of threefold expansion of private enterprise resulting in a higher rate of economic growth would make our tax burden lighter by making those who must bear it stronger. In fact, the first proposals of the administration in 1961 were to provide for tax reductions in the case of increased investment by business.

Is THE PRESENT tax burden equitable? Federal taxes today can be subdivided into three main groups: personal income taxes, taxes on corporate income, and various miscellaneous taxes—excise, estate, and gift taxes.

Personal-income tax collections now provide approximately half of federal budget receipts. Corporate income taxes are the next largest revenue source—about 25 per cent—and the miscellaneous taxes, including employment taxes, account for the other remaining 25 per cent of federal tax collections.

I believe there should be a general tax reduction without being too specific as to just where the taxes should be cut. "Get them down" is my motto so that we get total economic production *up* to yield not only enough revenues to balance the budget in this way by tax reduction, but "to advance the general welfare" as the Constitution calls for us to do.

A number of our tax experts want high-bracket rates reduced, so that persons with high incomes will be encouraged to take larger business risks and thus presumably create more jobs.

They have an interesting point, but the fact remains that a major deterrent to extreme socialism in any nation is the maintenance of a reasonably small gap between the wealthy and the poor. History has shown that when the gap becomes too wide, the poor —and in modern times, also the middle-income group—revolt. The graduated income tax which has prevented the rich from becoming too rich has been the salvation of the capitalistic, free-choice economic system. But a "soak the rich" tax policy can also be overdone; the bad effects of extremely high tax rates in the upper brackets are fairly obvious. High-income people are the main source of savings for economic growth in our society. If too much of their income is taxed away, society will lose in the long run because savings will not grow fast enough. Moreover, excessive taxes will discourage new and important, though usually risky, investment in small or beginning businesses. And the incentive for all to work at top performance is greatly reduced when the government takes too large a share of the financial reward for improvement.

Pursuing the question of whether or not the present tax burden is equitable, we must remind ourselves that our personal-income tax rates depend, at least in principle, upon our ability to pay. This is as it should be in a free society. Despite all the criticisms that can be made about loopholes and other deficiencies in our income and estate tax laws, there is no real question but that as a whole the existing structure is in fact highly equitable. Those who receive richer rewards for their efforts and those who inherit a greater share of worldly goods can properly be called upon to bear a greater proportion of the tax burden than those who do not.

But we must not carry the ability-to-pay principle so far that it becomes a mask for the practice of forcing the most productive and hard-working to carry the mediocre and lazy. If so, we will destroy incentives to greater production and efficiency and encourage dishonesty such as tax-dodging and income-hiding. The system of work and reward, the very foundation of strength for our free economic system, must be allowed to operate. If we place tax burdens on our most productive people and businesses so heavy that incentives and rewards are seriously weakened, for a short time the government may collect more in taxes, but in the long run and as a direct consequence, the government will have less income and property tax, and it will end up actually collecting less in taxes. Or if the government is determined to maintain its revenues, with fewer high incomes the smaller taxpayer will have to take on a larger share of the tax burden.

Actually, confiscatory rates on high-income brackets raise little for the government because there are relatively so few taxpayers, this in addition to the fact that these unreasonably high rates unduly penalize our most successful people. In 1957, for instance, the rates levied on taxable income above twenty thousand dollars a year yielded federal income taxes of about two and a half billion dollars—some 7 per cent of the thirty-five billion dollars collected from all individuals in that year. Or to put it differently, people with taxable incomes below twenty thousand dollars a year paid 93 per cent of all income taxes collected by the federal government. Even if the high-bracket rates had been cut in half, the total revenue loss would have been only about a billion dollars. Again, if one should wish to disregard the example of the rates levied on taxable income above twenty thousand dollars a year, the same argument can be used to cover the yield of tax rates over 50 per cent. The yield from these rates is less than one-half billion dollars. And had the rates in either of these cases been reduced, it is likely the government could have regained more than the lost revenue from economic growth in subsequent years.

WHEN I EMPHASIZE the importance to a free and healthy society of preserving incentives and rewards in the economy, I am not speaking merely as a man whose career has been in business. There is another important reason taxes should be kept low: the danger of hindering or even stopping the creation of jobs and of reducing purchasing power through overtaxation. I pointed out earlier that high taxes would discourage risk investment. This is also true of high, progressively graduated tax rates; they change the odds on taking business risks: the higher the tax rate, the less attractive investing in small business (for instance) becomes to the man with money to invest.

Take the theoretical case of a man who has a small factory that makes household utensils. One of the gadgets he has patented has become very popular. If he buys new equipment and modernizes his plant, he can cut his price, increase his sales, hire more workers, and make larger profits. But he is currently free of debt. If he buys more machinery and expands his operation, he will have to go back into debt. But going into debt again means risk and worry. He remembers vividly how long it took him and how hard he had to work to get to his present debt-free position. Also, he knows that a larger percentage of any increased profits, if he is lucky enough to make any from the new investment, will be taken away because he will be in a higher tax bracket. Under these circumstances, he may very well decide to sit back and not take the risk of modernizing his operation. Can you blame him?

Suppose he chooses not to take the risk because taxes have cut away the possibility of reward. The result is bad for our entire economy. There are no orders for new machinery. There is no price reduction on the product. There are no additional jobs for men to install the machines or operate them. If our gadget manufacturer has no incentive to expand his business, neither will thousands of other businessmen like him, and thus the entire society will suffer from a lack of normal business expansion. Consumers will not benefit from lower prices. Jobs will not be created and purchasing power will not be enlarged.

It is higher employment and a larger output and more jobs that we seek. One can in the foregoing paragraphs see how tax reduction for our businessman can produce many benefits for the total economy and the working groups. This is the great lesson we have to learn if we want to lower the amount of our unemployment.

AND NOW CONSIDER the difference for taxpayers between the first and the last dollars we earn during the year. The "bottom" dollars are worth considerably more to all of us than the "top" dollars, a result of graduated or progressive tax rates. This difference is very important—to us and to the economy of our country. The higher our incomes, above a rather low annual total, the larger the share of our top dollar that is taken by the government in taxes. Therefore, our top dollar earned is worth less to us because we have less of it left after taxes. As we work and progress up the income ladder, our incentive to do so is steadily reduced and eventually destroyed by a tax system that takes an ever-enlarging share of our top dollars. And unfortunately when we lose even some of our desire to strive harder and produce more, the nation loses, because it is on production that national well-being depends.

Besides their value being crucial in providing incentives, top dollars have another important function in our society. Our bottom dollars furnish the necessities of life; our top dollars enable us to build up the savings we can invest. If we take away our top dollars, we take away the very source of our investment funds. Moreover, when we consider the question of whether to make a particular investment, we consider the risk versus the return and incentives to invest become important. If we cannot earn a fair profit or return after we pay top-dollar taxes, we refuse to take the risk. Thus excessively high tax rates on top dollars discourage investment (particularly in new business), act as curbs on industrial expansion, and block an increased over-all national income. Therefore, living standards and the economic welfare of our people suffer when high taxes seriously weaken the value of our top dollars.

THERE ARE MANY other things we should consider in the tax programs that will have to be adjusted to meet the needs of the future. High on the list are the source of income and contributions.

1. Attention should be given to reducing the tax rates on wages and salaries or income from working. This would strengthen the incentive to work and progress. It would help to stimulate individual effort and productivity.

2. Then there is the matter of income-tax deduction for contributions. Our federal income tax laws permit contributions to religious, charitable, and educational institutions to be deducted from our incomes in computing our taxes. This is as it should be. Permitting these deductions promotes many truly worthwhile activities. One of these is scientific research. The United States fortunately has many citizens who have a combination of sufficient vision, enlightened public interest, and the farsighted financial means to contribute considerable sums to the advancement of science. A few years ago the tax laws were wisely revised—to the advantage of the nation—and the limitation was raised so that an individual can contribute an additional 10 per cent of adjusted gross income to schools and colleges, hospitals and medical and agricultural research organizations over the 20

per cent of adjusted gross income which can be contributed either to these same types of organizations or to other organizations in the charitable, scientific, educational, or religious fields.

Consideration should be given now, and near-future action taken, to proposals allowing even larger deductions for contributions to research in the field of science. Although the federal government has subsidized some scientific research—a realistic necessity today—I am convinced that this research can be conducted far more effectively by privately endowed institutions than by government bureaus financed as one by-product of taxation. Great discoveries come from much experimentation and varied approaches to the problems. And this variation is characteristic of our multiplicity of private research agencies.

ANY PROGRAM of tax reform should also include a re-examination of taxes on corporations, particularly with the end in view of more generous allowances for depreciation—which would encourage increased capital investment in industry. Other countries have long since recognized that liberal depreciation credit stimulates business investment, the all-important key to economic growth. In the United States, however, the combination of rising costs and rapid obsolescence—plus inadequate and unrealistic depreciation allowances for tax purposes—compels business to dip into accumulated earnings or borrow from outside sources just to replace worn-out or obsolete plants. More liberal depreciation allowances are badly needed to permit business to accumulate funds needed for additional expansion. Moreover, accelerated depreciation would provide an important incentive to new investment and industrial growth.

The existing tax structure is also onerous for the investor. There is double taxation of corporate earnings: first at the corporate level or source, again at the personal level or on the part of earnings which the stockholder receives as dividends. And double taxation here is an impediment to investment.

Some economists have even gone so far as to propose the complete abolition of taxes on corporate income. Were this to happen, personal income taxes would have to be adjusted upward to maintain total tax revenues for the government. However, personal incomes could also be enlarged by a requirement that the total earnings of corporations be taken into personal incomes, perhaps to the extent of 90 per cent, so that there would be a transfer from the flat and inequitable corporation income tax to taxing the same earnings at the fairly graduated personal income tax rates. In this way, there might result a modest increase in burden upon personal incomes, but the tax here is certainly much more equitable than is the flat corporate income tax.

There is no such thing as a tax on corporations. The corporation, defined as an invisible and intangible thing existing only in the contemplation of the law, can hardly be taxed. The taxes corporations pay now are either a deduction from the earnings of labor or a burden upon the price of the product (thus becoming a hidden sales tax), or a burden which so restrains economic expansion that its cost is seen in larger unemployment and the amount by which the economy fails to expand and grow to its potential.

We must remain on guard lest the corporate tax rate become so excessive that it will be detrimental to efficient business and to the exercise of good business judgment. In my opinion, to lower the present corporation rate somewhat would benefit the national economy over the long term.

ALTHOUGH MANY OF OUR present excise taxes or taxes on commodities and services are capricious, when economic conditions change excises do not vary in yield as much as income taxes do.

That fact is important to the government. For stability of revenue, excise taxes should continue somewhere near their present level and they should be more widely applied to additional goods and services. Because so many of our excise taxes fall capriciously on certain goods and not others, careful study should be made of our system of excises.

Objective research and study should also be made of our entire taxation system, with the purpose of eliminating inequities and simplifying the whole structure. Overlapping and inefficient administration should be eliminated, and compliance for the taxpayer should be made easier. This is of the utmost immediate importance for our national economy, and tax revision should be a priority order of business for the Congress. Incalculable productive power is being lost daily through the harassing struggle of individuals and corporations with "taxes," and other government regulations directly attributable to taxes. A complete overhaul of the present unwieldy and frequently out-of-balance set-up is overdue. When punitive federal taxation rates are combined with ever-increasing state, county, and municipal taxation, the results are destructive.

LIKE THOSE ON SOME OF the other subjects I deal with in this book, this chapter has raised more questions than it has answered fully. Taxation is a subject with which experts—the self-appointed and the real ones—have filled libraries. I have touched on some of the primary factors in taxation in our country today. If this discussion has helped some readers focus their faculties for re-examination and further thought, it will have served its purpose well.

At the beginning, I quoted Benjamin Franklin on "death and taxes"—neither one ever a completely comfortable subject. I also cited Justice Holmes' reminder that taxes are the price we pay for a civilized society. We are perfectly justified—and we have a duty—to be on watch for the dangers of suffocating taxation that can contribute to top-heavy government services and that can stifle individual initiative. But we have a society and a nation that, for all its faults, is the best yet in history. Americans should derive a deep satisfaction in paying fair taxes and thereby make our great country even better.

This curious and happy fact remains: after we have paid all of our taxes, we are still the richest people in history. After taxes, each American has more take-home pay than his counterpart in any other country on earth. After taxes, we enjoy greater security, more education, more social benefits, more private ownership, more freedom, and more individual opportunity than the citizens of any other country. Apparently taxation has not eliminated all the conditions for the good life. Indeed, taxation has permitted much good through government and has helped to add to the conditions for a better life.

When we pay our taxes, we are picking up the check for our share of the America we enjoy. It is sound practice to examine any check for errors or overcharging—but it is also a long-honored American practice to be proud to pay for value received.

SIX

LABOR AND MANAGEMENT

WE NOTED in looking at the interrelation and the parallel responsibilities of business and government in the United States today that it is much easier (and more comfortable) to stay on the surface of the subject and to accept without much examination the convenient stereotypes. This is certainly also the case when the subject at hand is American labor and management—perhaps more so than with any other two major interlocking segments of our society. Not only do the professional politicians and the spokesmen for special interests have a ready picture in mind when the two words are mentioned together; the general public also does. This stereotype, however, tends to read "labor *versus* management" and therefore avoids the crucial issue: the mutual responsibilities of labor and business to work together in keeping our economy strong.

In any serious discussion, the first important consideration is defining the principal terms. As I am using it in this chapter, *management* means business or industrial leadership and includes those individuals who either own or are directly responsible for guiding our system of private economic enterprise. Managers usually provide or obtain the capital, and in all cases must assume responsibility for success or failure of their venture. Management hires, directs, and coordinates men, materials, machines, and money; it has the equally important function of developing markets.

Labor as I am using the term here denotes all of our citizenry who (like businessmen or managers) are engaged in productive enterprise but who are in addition subject to management's direction and coordination. It includes all employees—the unorganized as well as those joined together in a labor union; white-collar and blue-collar, skilled and unskilled. I distinctly do not consider labor a marketable commodity, however, to be purchased whenever possible on cut-rate terms. My concept of a unit of labor is that of an American citizen engaged in an occupation he has chosen freely. And I have myself long been greatly concerned with the dignity of the worker as an individual—as I am with the dignity of every living human being—and with the human aspects of the relationship between employer and employee.

Management can purchase raw materials and the machines with which to process them. Businessmen can come to own and, within the law, do as they please with these nonhuman production factors. But management, in our system, cannot presume to own or command labor. Managers can only persuade and inspire, and successful persuasion requires that people be dealt with to their own advantage. Every man and woman in our tremendous labor force is first, last, and always a human being. He is not a machine or a commodity; he is an individual to be accepted and valued by management as such. For leaders to exist there must be followers. This may be a platitude but it is not a rationalization; it is a demonstrated historical condition of human society. For management to exist, to function, there must be labor. In our country and in our time, both are equally important partners in economic progress. Each must understand and respect the just needs of the other.

Businessmen need always to rate the human factor highest in their operations, and the most successful of them do. This leadership of men in economic enterprise is a striking challenge in human relations, and today an all-important challenge that stems from the need to inspire and motivate labor for the benefit of labor, of the whole society, and of the individual company.

NEVER BEFORE IN the history of the world has a labor force been so highly rewarded as ours now is in the United States. In 1960 wages for production workers in all manufacturing industries averaged more than ninety dollars a week, an increase of 260 per cent over the twenty-five-dollar-a-week average only twenty years earlier. We had inflation in the same period, but consumer prices rose less than half as much as wages—110 per cent. Thus, after figuring in the effect of rising prices, the 1960 average weekly wage bought over 70 per cent more than did the average 1940 wage. Stated another way, the purchasing power of the average production worker in our country multiplied more than 1.7 times between 1940 and 1960.

Actually, labor gained more than management did during this same twenty years. Total wages and fringe benefits for all employees in the United States increased by 242.3 billion dollars while corporate earnings before taxes increased only 35.7 billion dollars. During the same period, corporation taxes increased by 19.2 billion. Corporate profits after taxes thus increased far less —only 16.5 billion dollars during the same twenty years—and government took the larger share (54 per cent of 19.2 billion) of the total gain in corporate profits. In the two decades following 1940, labor income increased about fifteen dollars for every one-dollar increase in net corporate profits. Government income from corporations increased by just more than one dollar for each dollar left to corporations. This is the amazing record of private industry's ability to create incomes and wealth for both labor and government as well as for management. With the smallest share of the gain accruing to management, it is a remarkable record indeed for our free private-enterprise system.

A serious danger has developed in recent years, however, in the relationship among wages, productivity, prices, and profits. Wages have been rising faster than productivity since World War II. As a result labor costs have risen steadily, putting a tight squeeze on profits. Management has been forced to raise the prices of its products to maintain a reasonable and justifiable profit level—and the excess of wage increases over productivity increases has tended to produce inflation rather than goods.

We must stop such wage-price inflation. It is imperative for our economic health and therefore our national security that in the years immediately ahead we base new wage increases on productivity gains. In the past we have unfortunately not always acted wisely. In many instances labor leaders have forced up wages faster than productivity could grow. Some unions have forced management to accept labor contracts with "escalator" clauses which provide for automatic wage increases to compensate for increases in the cost-of-living index. The excessive wage increases alone have been bad for consumers, and therefore the vast majority of Americans, while excessive wage demands in combination with escalator agreements have been doubly bad in terms of promoting inflation. Experience has shown clearly that escalator agreements foster inflation because they gear wage increases to prices and living costs. If wages go up faster than productivity, prices rise. If prices rise, escalator agreements guarantee further rise in wages, which tends to push prices up once again. Thus continues a terrible upward spiral, with wages pushing prices and prices pushing wages.

Wage increases in any given firm should not exceed the average increase in productivity for all industries throughout the nation. This fact may very well not seem fair at first to those workers in industries in which productivity gains are above the national average. But only in this way can workers in below-average-productivity industries receive wage increases without causing inflation and permit all workers to share equitably in national productivity gains.

Even larger considerations are at stake. If strong unions in high-productivity industries are permitted to win wage increases above the national average increase in productivity, other unions in less productive industries will follow suit, and wage increases for the nation will rise rapidly above the national productivity average. As organized labor groups in industries in which productivity gains are not great press for wage increases to catch up with the wage gains of the powerful unions in the strong industries, the total wage-increase pattern for all industries is bound to be greater than the national increase in productivity and to result in cost-push inflation for the entire economy. In other words, costs will rise and it will become necessary for management to raise prices to avoid an unsafe drop in earnings. There are very few corporations today with such large margins that they can pay wage increases out of profits.

Another important reason for holding wage increases in all industries to the average increase in national productivity is clear with a better understanding of the economics of our profit-and-loss system. If wage increases everywhere do not exceed the average gain in productivity, profits will be greater in the highly productive industries and lower in the less productive industries. When this happens, our economic system will be permitted to function as it should: More capital will be made available for expansion of the highly productive industries from larger profits retained by these firms or from outside sources encouraged by the larger earnings. By the same process, investment will not flow into the less productive industries where profits are low, and these industries will not expand. This is as it should be: remember that profits as well as losses are necessary. For the proper functioning of our economic system, profits must appear;

they encourage the production of more of the goods we want. Losses must likewise be permitted; they discourage the production of goods we do not want. If all of the productivity gains are captured by labor unions in the form of higher wages, profits will disappear, industries will not expand, and we shall all lose—labor fully included—in the long run.

At this point the question of fairness and equity arises. Who is entitled to the productivity-gain benefits of American industry? Too often, without thinking we oversimplify and in the process overlook the whole story. The advantages of advances in productivity can and should be shared by three groups: (1) workers, in the form of higher wages, shorter hours, or both; (2) consumers, in the form of lower prices; (3) business, in the form of higher profits. All three groups—workers, consumers, and businessmen—have a right to a share of the gains. All the benefits of increased productivity should not go to labor, nor should labor wish all of them. Business furnishes the management skill and the risk capital, the new machines and tools, that contribute materially to our gains in productivity. Nor can we afford to forget to give to the largest group in our society, the consumer, a share of the benefits of rising productivity through lower prices. Think of what lower prices mean to all of us, and especially to the retired group and others on fixed incomes.

Wage policy is a national economic concern, and we must solve it before we can stop rising prices. Employers must do their best to help their workers understand that if prices are to be stabilized but wage rates are raised too rapidly, the resulting increase in costs and the consequent reduction in sales will result in eventual widespread unemployment.

WHETHER OUR ECONOMY can move forward from its present condition in harmony depends on the good intentions and the sensible actions of *both* management and labor. This does not for a moment mean we need to be frightened of encounters and debates between capital and labor; the only way to avoid them would be to shackle our freedom. Take away freedom and there is indeed no controversy—but then too there would be no free labor unions or free businesses.

Struggle is normal and healthy, but it can be contained in every successful family. Labor strikes are wasteful and the losses that result are never recovered by anyone; workers, the community of consumers, and owners all lose in one way or another. For the worker, strikes amount to self- or union-inflicted unemployment and loss of material well-being that is seldom regained. It therefore seems perfectly reasonable that workers should insist upon conciliation or even arbitration—with the public represented—when a strike threatens and management and labor cannot come to an agreement.

If labor and management are constantly at loggerheads in our free society, all of us as Americans face two distinct but equally grave threats to our freedom and to our security in the world. If a harmonious working relationship between management and labor cannot be achieved through the free exercise of their present rights, government will have to assume more and more control to maintain our economic strength and to keep things going. That would be an unfortunate necessity. It would slowly paralyze our free-enterprise system and deliver us to the domination of the state. And if industrial strife slows down our productive and technological advance, we will be at a serious disadvantage not only in meeting the Communist competition in the economic and ideological spheres but also in meeting friendlier but perhaps equally vigorous economic competition with other free nations.

MORE THAN A CENTURY AGO, during the industrial revolution in England, factory workers destroyed new machines because they feared the machines would replace them. Today some are worried that a modern technological advance, *automation*, will revolutionize production methods and cause unemployment. Technological progress is actually older than recorded history—it began with the cave man. Automatic machines have been in use for many years. The usable steam engine (and fly-ball governor to control it) goes back more than a century and a half—and the design for a steam engine of a sort goes back at least to the sketchbooks of Leonardo da Vinci. What we call automation today merely involves the employment of electronic and mechanical devices to keep material flowing from one automatic machine to another or to control the operations of those machines. Automation is simply another phase of technological progress—another stage in man's ceaseless effort to harness and utilize the forces of his environment, another expression of the climate of change and challenge of our time, and change and challenge in a free society amount to progress—something that free men need not fear.

While automation may well revolutionize a good many processes in industry, it is certainly not coming with explosive suddenness. It is developing gradually enough to permit us to adjust to the changes it will bring. The beginning stages of applied automation may indeed result in some temporary hardship for certain people; any change usually does. But automation is progress, and its advantages completely outweigh whatever problems it might bring. Automation permits the use of machines in place of men on hazardous or onerous jobs such as those in mines and foundries. It replaces men in dangerous work with explosives and radioactive materials. Automation also relieves man from unpleasant and tedious work, such as simple repetitive operations on assembly lines. Few today can honestly disagree that the substitution of machines for human labor on such jobs involves a gain to the worker himself, and most certainly all of society gains from this kind of progress.

Further, it is unlikely that automation will create any serious problem of unemployment. The slight and temporary unemployment, or dislocation in directly affected jobs, is predictable; they are therefore adverse effects that can be minimized. New installations can be planned far ahead of actual introduction and ample time thus be gained for reassigning or retraining the personnel who will be displaced.

Unquestionably the potential benefits of automation to the economy and to labor itself far outweigh the costs of any temporary dislocations. Although automation may take the place of some manpower, more manpower will be required to develop, build, operate, maintain, and direct the new devices and machines. Workers will still have to develop the products, plan the operations, and sell the output. The automobile, for example, created vastly more and better employment than it displaced. The auto industry requires men with higher skills and pays higher wages than was the case in the era of horse-and-buggy transportation. The age of automation will require even higher skills and more education, and happily it promises higher wages and an opportunity for better living. Automation will upgrade jobs of workers in both factories and offices.

One of our chief economic objectives remains, as it must, raising the productivity of all our labor. A larger product per man or per man-hour is the real source of gain in material well-being: both more leisure and higher wages. A rising standard of living depends entirely on rising productivity, and automation will help achieve this. More can be produced with less human effort and lower costs per unit. Automation will help bring about the high rate of productivity that America must have to keep our costs down and compete effectively in world trade. We must become the most efficient users of labor in the world, since we pay the highest wages in the world. Only by using less of our high-priced labor for each unit of product can we meet the competition of low-wage foreign goods. If we speed automation and lower costs, our foreign markets will expand; our exports will rise; national income and the individual incomes of our workers will grow. At the same time, our home markets will expand as we produce more and better goods at lower prices. Unemployment will dissipate and we shall all gain.

AFTER HE HAD BECOME an employer, Benjamin Franklin observed: "When men are employed, they are best content'd; for on the days they worked, they were good-Natur'd and cheerful, and, with the consciousness of having done a good day's work, they spent the evening jollily; but on our idle days they were mutinous and quarrelsome, finding fault with their pork and bread, and in continual ill-humor."

Franklin put his finger on the first and greatest social responsibility of business: to provide jobs. But his shrewd statement had implications that were true in his day and that are far more compelling in our society today—the responsibility of business beyond simply providing *some* kind of employment. Management must put labor to work doing the right thing, in the right place, at the right time. To guarantee a machinist the job of making buggy whips when buggy whips are not wanted is indeed wasteful and foolish and is certainly a poor attempt at offering job security. Management must put labor to work creating the goods and services consumers want and are willing to pay for. Business must show a profit—the reward for producing the right goods or services—before jobs can be truly secure.

As consumer tastes change and demands shift, the problem of assuring job security grows accordingly. Management cannot abdicate its responsibility, however; it must provide steady jobs for labor. In addition, business today in the United States must offer employees good wages, opportunity for advancement, and benefits above and beyond the pay for a day's work.

One of the great social challenges facing American business

today is finding ways and means to level off the peaks and valleys of the employment terrain. The desire for security on the part of labor is stronger today than at any time before in our history. This desire is the cause of much current labor-management strife. Union pressure for unrealistic "work rules" and "feather-bedding" to maintain jobs that no longer exist or create positions where there is no work is an attempt—though criminally and unpatriotically damaging to our economy—to gain job security. In demanding fringe wages, workers are saying—at least in part—that they want security and protection in case of unemployment, sickness, old age, or death.

But job security is a coin that, like all other coins, has two sides. Any employee's security is tied closely to the security of his company. This is elementary economics, but it is often ignored. Management must not forget that the desire of employees for security for themselves and their families is so deep-rooted and so strong that if business fails to provide reasonable security, employees will turn to government for it. And if labor is forced to turn to our politicians for security, we can expect they will get a large measure of their demands in return for their votes. That would inevitably mean more government control and bigger taxes for everybody, on top of increased costs and higher prices.

Just how far industry's responsibility goes in this matter of job security is still a matter of much discussion in business circles. There has been a considerable shift in thinking about this in recent years. No longer in our country—and a number of other countries in the free world—is it considered the responsibility of the individual and his family entirely to provide for old age, illness, and misfortune. Government has shouldered a share of the burden. Private industry also has accepted a large measure of the responsibility, as evidenced most clearly by the tremendous growth of fringe benefits and welfare plans in the past two decades.

Security *is* important. But in our search for it we must be careful not to lose sight of other equally important objectives. We must construct our programs for security so as to strengthen—not weaken—the corporation, the individual, *and* the total economy. And *the ultimate measuring stick remains productivity.* Unless the increased costs of programs to provide greater job security are accompanied by a compensatory rise in productivity across the board, these costs must be passed along to the consumer in the form of higher prices. If price increases are not possible businesses will fail, industry will be forced to cut back, employment will fall, and job security will not exist. Employee benefits are a part of costs; before an employee can expect more benefits, he must accept the corollary responsibility to increase his productivity.

BUT FOR EVERY HUMAN BEING, life is something more than the bread he eats and the means by which he earns that bread. Suppose an employee has a good income and a full measure of job security: is he content? No, he still wants something more. He craves satisfaction in his work and the respect of his fellows; he wants to feel that he is a member of a team.

These needs are much less tangible than wages and hours or pensions and insurance. But for management to ignore them is to invite discontent, inefficiency, and an underlying sense of frustration that cannot be eliminated merely by granting repeated demands for shorter hours and higher wages.

The desire of the individual for recognition and for participation is exceedingly important. Yet, instead of saying "Men, we are all on the team and we will win together," management has often seemed to say "Men, *I* am the team!" While management may only *seem* to say this and may think altogether differently, good thoughts—unlike good deeds—do not speak for themselves.

There are great differences between individuals. There are

similarities in terms of basic motivations, hopes, and fears, but no two human personalities are exactly alike. The desire for advancement is by no means universal. In the military services everyone knows there are distinct advantages in being an officer, yet many men prefer life as an enlisted man. The same is true in industry. Years ago, Henry Ford found that scarcely 5 per cent of his employees who wanted more money would accept any additional responsibility or a heavier work load to earn it.

Whatever the percentage of the ambitious today, it is vital that we keep open the door of opportunity for everyone so that those who do have the willingness and the ability to climb to higher levels can do so. An "open door" must always exist for every employee. I believe that equality of opportunity is a mighty weapon business shares with all Americans. We should use it against the critics and enemies of our nation. Offer opportunity to everyone. The man who wants it will make the most of it, and he will be a great booster of his company and of our American way of life.

THERE IS A great need for the invigorating and energetic force of good leadership, not only in business but in every phase of our national life. Vigorous, dynamic, and intelligent personal leadership is the determining factor in any institution—business, political, or educational.

Individuals in a company want strong leadership in their executives, and in every member of the management staff. They want delegated authority that permits not only second-level executives to exercise leadership but that gives any individual the opportunity eventually to become a part of management if he demonstrates leadership qualities.

Employees will work hard for management if they are convinced that by doing so they help themselves. An executive's primary function in dealing with his employees, therefore, is to lead, to motivate and inspire, to be fair, and to assure good human relations. Certainly capital investment in plants, buildings, and machines is important, but loyal and able men and women are the most important factor in making a successful company. Faithful employees with proved and tested enthusiasms and creative loyalty are the flesh and blood of any thriving organization. It is they who give the organization genuine strength and positive direction.

A full measure of efficiency and economy of operation, permitting a high-quality product to be sold at a low price and making possible good earnings, can be achieved only when employee morale and confidence in management is high. For the chief executive of a corporation, emphasis on good human relations is entirely consistent with his threefold responsibility: to his stockholders for adequate dividends and company growth; to employees for good wages, continuity of employment, and opportunity for advancement; and to the consuming public for good products and services at realistic prices.

The good industrial chief executive knows, in the words of Edmund Burke, "No men can act with effect who do not act in concert; no men can act in concert who do not act with confidence; no men can act with confidence who are not bound together by common opinions, common affections and common industry."

THE GREATEST GAINS in labor's productivity usually come not from work-load analyses and efficiency studies but from employees who are themselves interested in finding better ways to do their jobs. If workers are themselves motivated to produce more per hour, the result is lowering the labor cost per unit of production. This is the only lasting route to improving real wages. Furthermore, in the years immediately ahead of us, it will be impossible to obtain the national economic growth we must have

—and that we want—unless we have substantial gains in productivity per man-hour.

For a number of years the industry of the cities has been attracting people away from farms; in the past two decades some twelve million have moved from rural to urban areas. Today less than one tenth of our population is left on farms, and the cityward migration continues. At the same time, the record for productivity growth is higher in agriculture than in any other industry. Farm productivity per worker is higher than productivity per worker in urban industry. Thus, as farmers move from high-productivity agriculture they must join an equally high-productivity industry in the city; otherwise national average productivity will decline. This fact underlines the need for accelerating productivity in urban industry.

A good portion of modern personnel problems in our industry results from specialization and mass production. Under the older handicraft system, a man made an article from start to finish. He would look at the end product—the graceful silver teapot, the well-turned boot, the sturdy wagon—and know that his own strength and skill had made it. He took pride in his work, and he derived broad satisfaction from doing a good job.

Today much industrial work is monotonous, uninteresting. Frequently a pieceworker does not know the use of the part he makes. There is little meaning or purpose for him in what he is doing; little wonder he becomes bored. The worker doing a monotonous, repetitive operation today must have some compensation for pride of workmanship in the older sense. He needs recognition of some sort if he is to gain any real satisfaction from his job. It is up to management to find or devise ways of giving him this satisfaction.

Some years ago Western Electric, an electrical-equipment company, tried an interesting and successful experiment. A group of girls doing assembly work were placed in a separate room in which working conditions were changed frequently. The result was that production increased and absences decreased 80 per cent. The girls' attitudes changed and they were noticeably happier in their work.

The reason was not to be found in the changes in working conditions, the physical environment. It was the change in psychological environment that was really responsible for the high morale and the resulting increase in production. Before any changes were made the girls were consulted, their opinions asked, and they were invited to assist with supervision: They felt that they were taking part in an important experiment—as indeed they were. The work was as monotonous as ever, but the girls gained satisfaction from the fact they were being given consideration as individuals and that they were really participating in the business.

Many ways to increase the employee's feeling of participation already exist. Improved communication may help, for one thing. But whatever the particular technique adopted, the objective is clear. Management must work to improve individual employee understanding of what the whole company is trying to accomplish. Management in effect needs to lower the real or imagined barrier between itself and the employee.

The wise executive understands the motivations of human behavior and appreciates the basic needs of his employees as people. He makes certain that suitable recognition is given for outstanding work and that rewards are in keeping with the job performed. He takes his employees into his confidence and carefully informs them of company policies, rules, and regulations—and explains the reasons. A good boss must always seek to understand and to help his subordinates do a better job for themselves as well as for the company.

The degree to which business is successful in improving human relations within industry will determine the degree to which business will receive solid support and cooperation from all the members of the team.

I BELIEVE THAT American management is slowly but surely awakening to the fact that its employees have only a meager understanding of the economic forces under which they work and earn their livings. It is an important obligation of management to explain clearly to its employees—and, for that matter, to the whole public—the part business plays in modern American society.

It is not sufficient merely to repeat that management and labor are a team. Unless management gives its employees a complete picture of its operation—including finances—in terms every employee can understand, labor cannot be expected to act as a member of the team. It is up to management to take the lead in communicating and in developing understanding participation on the part of the employee.

In some instances, management will have to vault the barricade presented by a hostile union. But when truth is on its side and there are intelligent, objective foremen to interpret the facts, the management story can be brought home to the employees. The employee should always be shown how his wages and job security are directly tied to company earnings, and how both are in direct ratio to his productivity. This is unflinching truth, not propaganda. It is up to management to let its employees realize that they are in actual fact the most important asset of the company, to correct erroneous notions of excessive company earnings by showing the true relation of earnings to wages and taxes, to the sales dollar, and to investors' funds. Management must clearly and accurately show the importance of earnings and how profits are used for industrial and social progress. Management must reiterate—again and again—the facts that show how its employees have profited when the company has done well.

The worker who invests some of his earnings in the stock of his company gains a legitimate sense of belonging. He becomes one of the investors in his own productive efficiency. This is very much to the good, for the employee, the company, and the nation, and it should be encouraged. The fact that Americans in ever-increasing numbers are becoming stockholders in American enterprises, especially those enterprises in which they are employed, has led some economists to describe the American economic system as a working "Peoples' Capitalism."

An economic system that has produced the highest standard of living in the world does not have to apologize for its success. For its mistakes, yes, but not for its sucess. I believe that business is still not investing enough time and talent in the all-important job of showing its employees and the general public how the American combination of capital, management, and labor produces more goods and services than any other working combination in the history of the world.

This is an area too few Americans (not even to mention the rest of the world) know too little about, although it is one of the most vital and one of the most interesting factors of society in our time. And the truth gives a compelling opportunity for labor and management alike (and together) to take pride in our past successes and to see with greater clarity the abundant opportunities that wait to be realized.

SEVEN

BUSINESS AND THE COMMUNITY

THE WORLD of the twentieth century, the world we know and live in, is both debtor to and victim of the nineteenth-century economists. None of these economists—Karl Marx least of all —dreamed or understood that private industry could or would take the direction it has in the United States. Growing acceptance of broad responsibilities for the well-being of our whole society (and, increasingly, of a free world society) is the dominant characteristic of American business in the twentieth century—all accomplished within the framework of private capitalism. Thus Marx, an angry man and an idealist who predicted the destruction of private capitalism and for whom "dictatorship of the proletariat" was the ultimate end of all social and economic change, has been proved totally wrong.

Since the time of Marx the world has suffered enough to make every one of its thinking inhabitants frightened of the idea of dictatorship—whether of "the proletariat" or of individual tyrants. One sometimes wonders what sort of manifesto Marx would write today.

There are three dimensions to the social responsibilities now accepted by American business. The first and most important duty of the businessman is the provision for his employees of jobs and job security, opportunities for advancement, and an awareness of partnership in a worthwhile undertaking. Second is the production and sale at a fair profit of the goods and services that people need and want at prices they are able and willing to pay. Third is the use of profits for investment and growth so that society benefits again in the long term.

For quite some time businessmen have recognized the first and second responsibilities. However, provision of good employment opportunity is impossible unless the company can remain solvent—and that means producing high-quality goods that consumers want to buy. Thus these first two responsibilities of modern business, in my opinion, are inseparable and interdependent. The recognition of the third dimension of responsibility—the use of profits for the benefit of society—is coming with greater business maturity. In the early stages of the industrial revolution, and in the early history of our own nation, commerce was concerned primarily with itself, with maintaining high dividends, with building efficient organizations, with making and selling good products.

It is true that many companies, without openly announcing a sense of social responsibility, have made a great social contribution by improving the quality and reducing the price of their goods through increased productivity and greater efficiency of existing operation. Many more people have thus been able to buy and enjoy better goods and services, and the companies have reaped rewards in the form of larger profits. In this way the managers of such companies have helped others to better living, even though their motives were not altogether altruistic.

Undue concern for self in an individual and a corresponding inability to have concern for others is often the result of insecurity. Similarly, in business a precarious financial condition can blind a businessman to the broader concept of his responsibility to his society. As the business grows stronger and more mature, the businessman's view usually broadens. Today we must hasten this process. Happily, the businessman—if he becomes active in sustaining community well-being and supporting charitable organizations, if he helps advance the frontiers of science and supports education, if he works for a number of worthy causes—quickly begins to discover that both he and the community gain because of his unselfishness.

DEVELOPMENTS IN THE United States and throughout the world following the second world war have brought into sharp focus the absolute interdependence of the four major groups in our free-choice economic system: management, labor, stockholders, and consumers; spokesmen for each of these groups are admitting more and more readily the urgency of continuing cooperation if each is to continue to enjoy the fullest benefits of our way of life.

The modern corporation is by itself merely a few scraps of paper: a charter and by-laws, and some buildings equipped with tools and machines for production. It is human beings who give meaning, depth, and purpose to any corporation or business. *People* breathe into the company the social responsibility that has elevated our system to the high position it enjoys in the world today. The dignity and well-being of man is the true and ultimate goal of business leadership.

The social responsibilities of a business are fundamentally similar to those of an individual. The individual's primary responsibilities are to his family group and his community. The responsibilities of a business extend to its employees, stockholders, customers, suppliers, and to the communities in which it operates. For Americans—individuals and businesses—these responsibilities have come to extend beyond the nation and to encompass the world. Just as society expects more and more of the individual as he benefits from the fruits of our dynamic economy and from group living, so society justifiably expects more and more of business. These greater responsibilities are in direct ratio to the benefits and greater opportunities made possible by over-all economic growth and the development of mass markets.

While business in this country still operates for the most part in a free-market system, it is worth noting here that almost every instance in which the free market has been limited by government the limitation has been imposed to compel business to accept social responsibilities it has shirked in the past. Consider our social-welfare legislation, our antitrust laws, our minimum-wage laws. These and a number of other government measures in our recent history have been attempts to legislate social responsibility that could conceivably have been assumed without such measures by earlier cooperative, farsighted industrial leadership.

MODERN AMERICAN CAPITALISM must willingly make innovations to meet changing conditions if it is to surmount the Communist threat. Both the Russian and the Chinese interpretations of communism are changing with the times; both are steadily making adaptations. But they have a single goal: the over-riding objective of communism—completely to dominate the world—has not changed.

American industry, and industry throughout the free world, must begin answering articulately and intelligently the questions men and women are asking quietly in their homes or loudly in public. Here are only a few of the many: Is industry planning far enough ahead to be able to provide jobs for our rapidly growing population? Is business giving equal opportunity—regardless of artificial factors: race, creed, or original nationality—to everyone willing to work? Is business providing job opportunities for our handicapped citizens, who are capable of being employed in many lines of work? How much of its profit is industry plowing back into research and investment so that the public can have better products and better services and a steadily rising standard of living?

I am certain that any company today that will take the trouble to explain its operations honestly and thoroughly—not only to its stockholders, but also to employees and to the general public —will be well along the way toward eliminating much of the unfair or false criticism leveled against it and against business as a whole. A company that is a good "corporate citizen" in our society is one that produces a good product at a reasonable price, one that pays its employees fairly, rewards its owners with a reasonable return on their investment, and plans for the future with new and better products to improve our standard of living. The story of such a good corporate citizen provides the best possible testimony for American business and our way of life. It moreover furnishes the powerful weapon of truth against the enemies of freedom. There is no conceivable justification for hiding our bright light under a bushel in these times in which the challenge is so great and the enemies of freedom so strong.

To accomplish anything of lasting value in the relationships between business and society, the program must be honest, continuous, and extend over a long period of time. Dr. Samuel Johnson once said "A man, Sir, should keep his friendships in constant repair," an admonition that might have been addressed to business today. Good will cannot be written on the books overnight, and it can never be written to stay without regular subsequent entries. All ink tends to fade in the ledger of public opinion. Additional entries must be made daily.

AN EXECUTIVE in a large American corporation today has an unusual opportunity to observe the workings of economic forces and to gain an excellent understanding of what makes our economy tick. It is his obligation not only to see that his company renders a public service by efficiently producing and distributing quality products and providing employment, but also to share his knowledge and understanding with others. Thus the broader responsibility of a business executive as a statesman is to assist directly in the development of an increasingly productive and prosperous national economy.

In our free and competitive economy, management must act as a balance. It must mediate the sometimes conflicting interests of employees, stockholders, and the consuming public. Management is in a position of trusteeship for each of these groups, insuring that no one group gains unreasonable advantage at the expense of the others. The work of management in providing balance has intensified with the cleavages that have appeared between these groups and the growing power of one group—labor unions.

Seventy-five or a hundred years ago, the average business firm was small and was usually owned by one man or by a partnership of two or three. The office was probably a corner of the shop or mill, and the business was managed by an owner who knew personally every man who worked for him. The proprietor thus combined in himself the functions of management and ownership. He was, moreover, closely identified with labor.

In our present society, management has become more and more an entity separate from both ownership and labor. Yet its obligations to both—and to the public—are more important than ever. Businessmen who are economic statesmen, not mere slaves of the balance sheet, are badly needed today. As American industry has grown, the welfare of millions of stockholders, employees, and consumers is involved in the day-to-day decisions of the manager. And further growth promises greater responsibility.

The American public wants leadership in industry to speak out. I believe that everyone in the world of commerce must now make whatever contribution he can to the solution of the major problems of the day. What are the aims and needs of the country? Are there weaknesses or failures in our present system? What are the policies industry should adopt and follow? If

American businessmen will speak out on these and similar questions, we shall in time arrive at a workable agenda for the future, an agenda that will help bring us the unity we so sorely need in this critical period of world history.

GOOD CORPORATE CITIZENSHIP requires that a business be public-spirited and willing fully to carry its share of charitable and welfare responsibilities in society. In many corporations it is now an accepted custom for officers and employees to take an active part in community organizations. Businessmen serve on hospital boards and conservation committees and sponsor Junior Achievement programs for training young people. Whenever necessary they are allowed time off during business hours for these activities.

I believe that our own time and energy are just about the most valuable contribution we can make, individually, to the community. Backing up financial support with personal participation in the work of a cause helps the most and is always desirable. As Lowell said in "The Vision of Sir Launfal,"

> Not what we give, but what we share,
> For the gift without the giver is bare.

Although corporate social responsibility is widely recognized in business today, the amounts corporations should give to charity, education, and other community services continue to be a subject of considerable debate. A single definite figure is difficult to determine and must, of course, depend upon the individual circumstances that affect each company. Some businessmen favor giving the full 5 per cent of earnings (taxable income) our tax laws permit to be deducted. Others give less; at present the aggregate contribution of industrial corporations is much less.

If corporations gave the full 5 per cent, two billion dollars would be available for worthy causes annually. However, no responsible board of directors can set up a program for giving away 5 per cent of a company's profits unless they are convinced they are putting the money in the right place and that it is good business to do so. Management must be prepared to justify its action to stockholders and employees, to the public, and to government.

Unfortunately, the need for charitable donations is usually greatest during economic recession, when business profits are small and corporations are as a result least able to give. As one way of equalizing gifts from year to year and giving more when the need is greatest, an increasing number of corporations are establishing foundations for contributing to the charitable and educational institutions of our society.

IT IS ONE OF the responsibilities of business in this peoples' capitalism of ours to encourage more individuals to participate in the rights and privileges and the obligations of company ownership. There is no more effective way by which industry can strengthen the economy and underwrite our way of life. People who own a share of American industry are more eager to protect the legitimate interests of business and more willing to defend our free-enterprise system against its enemies. Broadening the base of business ownership through wider sales of stocks and bonds anchors business more firmly to the public interest and encourages more enlightened public concern with business problems. At the same time, sale of stock to employees helps create better working relationships between management and labor.

Every man to own a few shares can become a new and powerful feeder stream into the American economy. The 1959 Census of Shareowners made by the New York Stock Exchange showed that between 1956 and 1959 the number of individual share-holders in this country increased by 45 per cent to a total of nearly twelve and a half million people—almost double the number of shareholders in 1952. But contrast that figure with the thirty-two million people who now own U.S. Savings Bonds. Much more can be done in broadening the base of industrial ownership.

There are many false impressions about stock ownership. Surveys have revealed that almost one third of the American people believe that only a handful of such people as the Du Ponts, the Rockefellers, and the Fords own most of the industry in America. Eight out of ten admit they have no idea of the number of people who jointly own a big corporation, and one person in five guesses that big corporations are usually owned by fewer than a hundred stockholders.

The more we encourage the small investor, the more will our system attain the stability that comes from a broad base set down in the bedrock of all the people of America. More widely scattered stock ownership will give these new capitalists a fresh and deeper insight into the problems of industry. It will help promote national policies creating a favorable climate for American industry—for all America.

The problem is clear: More people need more of a direct interest in our dynamic and free economy. To become really interested and concerned, people require a sense of ownership, of participation. The people of America must become strong advocates of our private-enterprise system of American business, which is another way of saying they must become more freedom-conscious. Our average citizen needs to stake out his private claim in the venture capital which keeps America forging ahead. When he owns a few shares, he increases the productive capacity of our economy while, at the same time, he builds his personal security.

ALTHOUGH BUSINESS is beginning to do a fair job of selling itself and our industrial system to the public, there is much left to be done. The goal toward which all Americans are working is a simple one: the survival of freedom and a better standard of living. The goal of business is identical with that of the average man. The job is to convince the public of the truth of this simple statement, because it is the truth.

The place for each company to start is with its own stockholders. The progressive and intelligent stockholder wants management to treat him as an owner and a partner in the enterprise, not merely as a name on the stock records. And this feeling of participation and concern on the part of the stockholder is something progressive management wants to encourage. Unfortunately, however, there are also many apathetic stockholders. They stay away from annual meetings in droves, and few ever visit their companies or write letters to the officers.

It therefore becomes an additional duty of management to try to awaken in its stockholders the responsibilities of ownership. Of course the best way to arouse the interest of stockholders is by friendly personal contact, frank and unimpeded two-way communication. More and more corporations are making their annual stockholders' meetings an interesting experience for those who attend. Top management and directors are present to welcome stockholders; reports are dramatically presented; progress is described; products are exhibited and explained; after the meeting, management, directors, and owners socialize together.

The annual report is the most important of the documents prepared for stockholders. During the past two decades company reports have evolved from the dry and complicated financial statements of yesteryear into modern, readable, interesting reports. This is a long step in the right direction. These reports should include a clear presentation of management philosophy and of major problems and current situations in labor relations. They should be full of news about the development of new products, facts on plant expansion, advertising, and public service.

An all-important supplement to the written annual report is the report given in person. That was the philosophy of James F. Bell, the late founder of General Mills, when he inaugurated the custom of holding informal regional stockholders' meetings as long ago as 1938. In the eleven years I was chairman of the board of directors, I had the privilege of conducting, every other year, General Mills regional stockholders' meetings in some ten cities throughout the nation. On each of these trips I also conducted mock stockholder meetings at two different universities in order to assist in educating the students concerning corporate relations between management and owners. In the fall of 1959, General Mills inaugurated another new custom by concentrating the regional stockholders' sessions in one afternoon, every other year, connecting by closed-circuit television the cities where the stockholders are gathered. These meetings have proved most effective in promoting understanding.

Questionnaires are also of value to management in learning what subjects are of greatest interest to stockholders. My own experience with such a questionnaire showed a gratifyingly large response and a wide range of interests. First in interest for stockholders of General Mills were our new products, new facilities, research, and plans for the future. Next came profits and the financial outlook. Then came current problems facing the company, followed by company policies and the reasons for them, and finally the company's current products and services. One out of every five stockholders took the trouble to give us some additional suggestions and comments as well as to answer all the questions.

MORE AND MORE, business is becoming conscious of its larger responsibilities to the national and international society in which it operates. Small business must of necessity limit its activities to a restricted locality, but it should strive to make its own community a better place to live. National corporations have broader obligations. They have a responsibility to each of the many communities in which they have plants and offices. They also have a duty to provide leadership and assistance on a national scale.

Those companies which operate internationally have a still more extensive obligation. In the interests of both patriotism and profit, *in that order,* they must conduct their operations in a manner beneficial not only to the companies themselves but also to both the United States and the other nations in which they do business.

Business has a responsibility through the corporations that conduct operations abroad to make certain that employees overseas project the best possible image of our country. They should become a part of the community in which they live and participate extensively in its activities. Knowledge of the local language is essential. Equally important is an understanding of the culture and motivations of the local people.

The success of a business venture is generally in keeping with the service it renders the society in which it operates. This is fully as true of operations in foreign lands as it is in our own country. And good labor-management cooperation demonstrated abroad is a constant object lesson to the rest of the world on how well our way of life and free-enterprise system operate from day to day, to the benefit of all.

EIGHT

EDUCATION: THE RACE
FOR INNER SPACE

"OUR FUTURE will be decided not in outer space but in inner space, the space between the ears."

In this era of unparalleled change and challenge there is almost universal agreement on the necessity of an educated world citizenry. Revolutionary developments in science and technology have triggered far-reaching economic, cultural, and psychological reactions among the world's peoples. Today's international tensions are both frustrating and frightening because they contain such profound possibilities for future good or tremendous evil. Even so, ours is an age of rising expectations: individuals and nations are struggling against poverty and seeking to find mutual working principles for world harmony, and we are beginning to realize that the future belongs to the educated man. With him, we may be able to save ourselves. Without him we cannot.

We have in operation the biggest and the best public school system in history. We possess great universities, hundreds of excellent colleges, and a rapidly growing program of vocational and adult education. Within our school plants, the majority of them modern and well equipped, are educators who are willing to devote their time, energies, and imaginations to teaching or administration at a salary level lower than most of them could command in other professions or in industry. A constant search for better techniques and media for teaching is going on, and every year there is an increasing tendency on the part of business to aid education, particularly at the higher levels.

Free public education has been part of the American tradition since the colonial period, and distinguished still-active institutions of higher learning founded well before the American Revolution include Harvard, Yale, Columbia, and the College of William and Mary.

No one in the history of this country has been more articulate about or demonstrated a clearer understanding of the meaning of the American way of life than Thomas Jefferson. Yet when Jefferson dictated the epitaph for his tombstone, he chose to describe himself as the father of the University of Virginia and as the author of the Declaration of Independence and the Statute of Virginia granting religious freedom rather than as a statesman, philosopher, and former President of the United States.

In the Jeffersonian tradition and the belief that where there is no education there can be no true political freedom, we in the United States have continued to build great state universities and land-grant colleges and to support and enlarge privately endowed schools. These institutions, in Abraham Lincoln's words, are by the people, of the people, and for the people. The citizens collectively pay the bills; donors provide the support; and all receive the benefits of these strongholds of freedom, intellect, and inspiration which are also increasingly becoming centers of scientific research for human betterment in every respect.

I NOTED EARLIER that the future now belongs to the educated man. But what is an "educated" man or woman in today's complex world?

The professional definition-makers have written weighty books in an effort to explain education. For too many people, however, *educated* still merely means possession of a college degree or a string of degrees. Earned degrees are, of course, the evidence of a period of formal education—often garnered at the cost of great devotion and personal sacrifice—and many who possess one or more of them are genuinely educated human beings. But the definition-makers tend to confuse the basic facts and the mere degree-seers tend to oversimplify.

In simple terms, real education is the process of continuing mental, spiritual, and practical growth in any person. Indeed, the ingredients include formal education, but the extent of classroom work and meeting of residence requirements varies widely. Today, the adequately educated citizen is the man or woman who is alert to the world and is engaged in lifelong learning (or educational growth) on two major fronts. First, he has or is seeking a practical understanding of modern science and technology and thus is able to see what they can do for his society. Second, he is alert; he seeks constantly to be able to evaluate present change and challenge in terms of human progress. This requires a sense of moral values and some acquaintance with what have traditionally been called the humanities: history, languages, the fine arts, philosophy, economics, sociology, psychology, political science, and religion.

The educated man is also able to establish satisfying and meaningful relationships in his everyday life; since he is able to put together a good many of the pieces that make up both past and present experience, he tends to be both more mature and less fearful—a point we shall return to in a moment.

To put it another way, education can truly liberate a man, freeing him for great accomplishments. Education in this sense becomes the way in which an individual acquires the knowledge and the understanding necessary to make wise decisions for himself, the decisions that first lead to satisfying and constructive relationships within his family and his community and then enable him to participate as part of that community in building a broader cooperative stability throughout the world.

Our word *educate* stems from the Latin verb that means "to lead forth." Education in its full sense prepares men and women to lead, surely one of the noblest functions of free men in a free society.

If we accept in substance this concept of what education is, we may then properly ask what education can be expected to *do* for a free citizen in a country that believes in freedom. I have suggested one answer: it prepares him to lead.

An interesting statistic furnishes another answer. Today only about 1 per cent of the skilled, better-educated group of our population is unemployed, against a 10-per-cent unemployment figure among the unskilled group. Obviously education pays in a material way. The more vital point, however, is the fact that people who do not or cannot develop themselves through education today are underemployed—something that harms both them and our society.

Still another important answer, I believe, is this: the better the educational development of his potentialities, the greater an individual's emotional maturity and intellectual stability. The better a person is educated, the more at peace he will be with himself and the better adjusted he will be in the world.

The educated person, in the relatively simple but sound definition we are using here, can much more readily avoid an unconstructive reaction to the psychic shocks that come so often with change and that are the roots of personal and mob hysteria based on fear. The educated man or woman—or the educated society—is better able to accept new techniques and discoveries without discarding what is valid in the cumulative experience of the past. They are equipped through education to re-examine the contributions of the past and relate them to current knowledge and need for action. To the extent to which his individual capacities of this kind have been "led forth" by education, the educated person can be a partner in shaping human progress, and the educated society will be a full partner in making the history of its epoch.

Education not only prepares us to lead; it also helps us to be good followers by giving us a respect for complexity and an appreciation for competence. Many of us are—and should be—leaders in our own specialities; in other areas, much of the time most of us are and should be followers. It is quite as important to be a discriminating follower as it is to be a good leader. The one cannot get along without the other. This is what is meant when it is said that we have to have great audiences to produce great artists, or that a people gets leadership determined in large part by the quality of its "followership"—what the constituency demands and expects.

SINCE EDUCATION IS of such vital importance to our present and to our hopes for the future, it would seem that members of the teaching profession should enjoy greater prestige in our society than they now do. More of us should make a stronger effort to recognize and understand the problems with which they are daily confronted, and we should support measures that will afford for teachers a better living standard than present overall wage scales allow them.

This is a two-way street, however. While the general public needs to show its understanding and appreciation of the devotion of most educators, the members of that profession have a responsibility to become more fully aware of the needs and the functions of the community in which they work.

The obligation of the educator is not merely one of disseminating knowledge and accumulated experience, important though this is, but also to train individuals to think—to be self-reliant and fearlessly open-minded in their quest for knowledge —and to inspire them ceaselessly and to tirelessly search for the truth, wherever it may be found and whatever it turns out to be.

Within the framework of the community—the neighborhood, the city, or the world—the educator must ask far more than unquestioning conformity on the part of his students, much more than blind adherence to established patterns or accumulated knowledge of the past from books and lectures. The great achievements in the arts and in science have come throughout human history from those who have developed fresh ideas and who had the courage to test those ideas.

The educator has a tremendous opportunity and responsibility in our time, and he deserves our appreciation and support.

IN AN AGE that requires frequent shifts of emphasis and almost constant critical re-examination of accepted methods of doing things, education faces its newest obligation. Until the recent past, our universities have been comfortably regarded as institutions intended principally for the instruction of youth. We can now no longer expect to survive, or even to "keep up," if we depend solely on the leisurely education of our youth and if we accept a more-or-less arbitrary cut-off point at which education is considered finished. Higher education must be for the middle-aged and the older as well, those who are already in responsible positions of leadership. A start in the right direction has already been made, and our institutions of learning are beginning to make their facilities much more widely available to a broader segment of the population. But so far it is only a small start.

It is no longer enough that a small number in our society is approaching or has achieved intellectual maturity. The greatest possible proportion of our people must help in the re-examination of human problems and the reassessment of values, particularly in the presence of continuing psychological and scientific discoveries. We must keep on raising an army of alert and perceptive men and women; we must also have a vast "ready reserve" of the intellectually mature, citizens whose formal *and* informal education continues unabated.

Although it is a truly important one, this is not a revolutionary suggestion when one remembers the changes that have been dictated by the needs of progress and civilization—even the struggle scarcely more than a century ago in the United States to include the so-called natural sciences in the curricula of our universities.

Our colleges and universities today must advance and grow better to serve the pressing needs of America in the years ahead. Without losing their ability to furnish their full-time students the best of academic and technical educations, they must expand unceasingly as centers of scientific research for human betterment in all respects, remain the advance guard of intellectual effort, and grow stronger as the special fortresses of freedom they are uniquely equipped to be. Our free society provides the climate and can provide the material support in which our colleges and universities may flourish and grow in freedom; the universities and colleges in turn must provide place and opportunity for the citizens of that society to learn the ways of freedom—to innovate and practice, to discuss and defend the right to discuss.

Our colleges and universities must constantly seek ways to inculcate a genuine understanding of our country's fundamental values and unchanging beliefs; they must also discover ways to broaden interest in and knowledge of international affairs among an ever-greater percentage of Americans. The era of isolation for America is gone forever.

Less than ever before can we afford to take for granted the security of our way of life. No longer can international affairs be considered simply chance relationships between nations, like billiard balls colliding on a table. They are now more complex interchanges and relations between entire peoples, blocs of nations, and individuals. Today the internal affairs of the people of one country are likely to be the concern of the people of another country. What happens in an underdeveloped area on the "other side of the globe" has repercussions in Iowa; what happens in Berlin affects what happens in Boston—and vice versa. What happens in Montgomery, Alabama, U.S.A., is known by millions of people throughout the world.

OUR RELATIVELY SIMPLE DEFINITION of education included the fact that it is a continuing process, a lifetime involvement. One of the principal purposes of continuing education—after high school or after college or after interrupted formal schooling at some earlier point—is to deepen our personal understanding of the great ideas that are the girders of our own heritage: justice and equality for all; freedom and responsibility of the individual; the rule of law; and the rights to life, liberty, and the pursuit of happiness. A long lifetime is scarcely enough for even the greatest minds to master the significance of such concepts. For the rest of us, who also have to earn our living and raise our families and devote much of our energy to the concerns of business, the process must be constant in the time we can give to it. We have, particularly in these challenging days, a need to understand the history of our nation and the history of mankind— and both of these are not only constantly becoming better known but are also constantly being reinterpreted.

Education in its fullest sense therefore can help every person develop in himself an increased participation in all the experiences of mankind everywhere. In organized groups or individually, through the study of the fine arts, of history, literature, philosophy, science, and religion each of us may learn to appreciate the struggles of mankind in its never-ending quest for knowledge and fulfillment. Today, when it is an inescapable obligation for the individual citizen to understand his own and other cultures, an acquaintance with the long chronicle of man and his endeavors provides an invaluable basis for comparison and evaluation.

Our continuing education deals with the most important questions of personal life. Since the individual, not the state, is the unit of measurement in a free society, our interest in individual development—our own and that of others—cannot be terminated at a specific time during our life; and most certainly not at the moment of graduation from high school or from college. Education throughout life is far more than merely a matter of facts and figures, or of formal book learning in or out of classrooms; it involves meanings, values, ethics, and morality in the widest sense. Human dignity and the sanctity of the individual cannot be considered apart from man's spiritual nature and his intellectual and economic characteristics. Sometimes these spiritual and religious traditions seem relatively unimportant to the young; this is another reason genuine education is a lifetime process, because with maturity these issues begin to take on for individuals the great importance that is implicit in them.

In addition to the growth of organized adult education programs, there has recently been in operation a movement toward the coordination of institutions and agencies concerned with the education of adults—in other words, with continuing or lifetime education. For a decade the Fund for Adult Education has been making a real contribution in encouraging the movement, but much still remains to be accomplished. On its side, the university must move toward a better integration of its own relation with the adult community around it, so that it does not have merely a general extension program or an agricultural extension program, or a program for doctors or lawyers or engineers. What is much needed now is some kind of coordinated method for using the resources of the great university or the distinguished college practically and actively to help the community in which they are situated and which they were established to serve.

THE NEED FOR this workable interaction between educational institutions and the community is heightened because our country is moving toward what a prominent educator has called "the educative society"—one in which the entire society and all of its components are concerned with the effect they are having upon individuals now and what that effect will mean to the generations ahead.

In the full-fledged educative society it will not be possible to compartmentalize education into bits and chunks. In a self-governing society—especially in one of constantly accelerating change, as ours is today—education takes on proper perspective as a continuing process, both for the adults and for their children, not as something to be endured in childhood and youth, then forgotten as adult responsibilities and interests are taken on.

Probably one of the greatest benefits of this concept to our over-all society is the fact that it helps create greater—that is, more complete—equality of opportunity. We begin better to provide, for all, fully equal opportunity to become educated while we supply at the same time the facilities which enable the especially talented to forge ahead at their own pace. The only automatic human equality, remember, is in infancy. Thereafter, levels of attainment depend to a great extent on individual capacities and effort. It must naturally follow that since we are unequal in our native gifts of strength, mentality, and motivation, we are unequal in our maximum individual capacities for development. Equality of opportunity in education will assure each human being freedom to develop his own potential to its limit.

IT HAS SURELY BECOME CLEAR, even during this brief discussion, that our concepts of education are being forced to change. In the early history of our Republic, while the world appeared to be changing only slowly, "vertical" education was usually sufficient; it was enough for the somewhat more mature to teach the immature as best they could. On the frontier, particularly as the young nation moved westward, often the only teachers available were young men and women scarcely older than their students, whose book learning was often only a few jumps ahead of that of their brightest pupils. Even so, such teaching was far better than no organized education at all, and laid the foundation for the lifework of many successful and productive Americans. Since the world remained substantially unchanged through their lifetimes, it was sufficient for a few generations to learn in childhood and youth all they could, and all they needed to know.

Now vertical education is no longer adequate, and "lateral" learning must give the traditional way an added dimension. Lateral education is education based on the realistic assumption that the world as we know it will continue to change and that the change and challenge will continue to build up. To keep up and to contribute, we must learn from each other and we must never stop learning.

No longer can any of us consider himself truly educated by merely sifting and assimilating the collected knowledge of the past, handed down to us by our elders, accepted without question and learned by rote. Businessmen, professional people—all, both young and old—must now learn better how to benefit continuously from lateral and continuing education through steady interchange of ideas and methods as they are developed and refined by specialists, all through our lives. And we must in return be willing and eager to teach, laterally and vertically.

ONE OF THE EDUCATIONAL CHALLENGES of our time is the need for day-to-day improvement in the quality of formal education as it is offered by our schools and colleges, excellent though these may be at any given point. Particularly in higher education, the curriculum, teaching methods, and the quality of the faculty personnel must keep pace with the obvious and implicit demands of these days. This means accelerated improvement in all areas. Even if it feels the temptation, American education simply cannot afford to rest on its achievements of the past. Our nation today requires much more.

It has seemed to me for a long time that we Americans simply take for granted the smaller educational institutions which have contributed so much to the greatness and growth of America. We tend to pay our respects to the large universities, nationally recognized, and often completely overlook the smaller institutions—the privately endowed schools, the small liberal arts and denominational colleges—who collectively have contributed as much as their larger counterparts.

Often the smaller, relatively independent college can act swiftly and efficiently to innovate, improvise, and originate new approaches when change is required. Since the smaller colleges are frequently in a better position to experiment and to take the lead in pointing new ways for larger schools and state universities, our smaller units serve to stimulate the whole system. The result is greater excellence in higher education.

Moreover, in our smaller institutions of higher learning there is a splendid academic standard, the opportunity for social growth within smaller student bodies, and the chance for individual exchange between student and professor which is so frequently the spark that lights the flame within a youth and sends him searching for knowledge—and sharing it—for the rest of his life.

EDUCATION TODAY HAS BECOME a gigantic business. But in spite of the size, American higher education does not have the capitalization found elsewhere in big business today. Our colleges frequently and necessarily present the picture of living practically hand-to-mouth. For small and large colleges alike to continue and expand their vital functions, it is becoming more and more apparent that there must be a dynamic partnership between education and industry.

I am repeating the obvious when I say again that our standard of living in the United States is, nationally, the world's highest. We like it this way, and we are seeking both to continue to raise the average standard and to assure that every citizen has the opportunity to partake of the comforts of that standard; this is the goal and the task of industry. To do this we must have a recurring supply of leaders for every important position of supervision. Business today can find technical specialists more easily than it can broadly educated and well-rounded men and women with leadership ability. More and more, industry is looking to the country's colleges and universities for its potential executives as well as for its specialists. A closer liaison and cooperation between industry and our schools would bring forth a greater number of better-qualified leaders for business and would work to the mutual advantage of industry and education.

Business should support education, then, in the first place because of what is often called "educated self-interest." It needs leadership personnel. It also needs qualified research personnel; we now know that economic growth and improvement of the American economy depend largely upon the constant expansion of research in every field. Engineering research gives us better products and better ways of producing them. Research in the general area of industrial human relations aids in the creation of a more satisfying work day and in the development of a labor force that will steadily become more efficient.

Equally important is research in medicine and in pure science as modern technology and exploration disclose more facts about our environment. In medicine we already have striking examples of what can be accomplished when professional and educational activities are closely associated; this is an area, too, in which industry has contributed fairly extensively, with the result that both education and business have profited. The same sort of thing should—must—be encouraged in business schools and the business community. Schools of business and economics, with the backing and encouragement of industry, should enlarge research leading to the improved techniques necessary for industrial progress in addition to their present detailed special instruction in accounting, financial management, market analysis, among other subjects. Their curricula could—and should—also give more attention to the broader area of business' responsibility to the whole society.

Education in America has a current annual budget of nearly twenty billion dollars, with more employees and more extensive facilities than any private industry. In a sense, this is still the beginning. We are barely starting to see the effects of the heretofore unprecedented numbers of our people who need education. The Council for Financial Aid to Education estimates that college enrollment, now at 3.8 million, will reach at least 6.5 million by the end of this decade. To provide for this tremendous increase, America's expenditure annually for higher education, now 5.4 billion dollars, will be well over 9 billion dollars by 1970.

We are just beginning to learn that investment in education of our people can create as good an earning asset as industry creates by investing in new plant facilities. Professor T. W.

Schultz of the University of Chicago, in his recent presidential address at the annual meeting of the American Economic Association, reported his studies had led him to the conclusion that not more than half of our gains in industrial productivity for a large number of years could be explained by investment in new plant facilities and that improved education and trained skills in our people would explain a great share of those gains.

The public school system is one aspect of the big-business picture of American education today, but in many respects this is a public trust; let us concentrate here on the relationship between higher education and industry, except to point out that industry's cooperation with public education is extensive, varied, and imaginative.

In the world of education, as in the business world, it is axiomatic that a college must operate efficiently and give maximum service for the least possible cost. Today our institutions of higher education are being hampered by the need for additional operating capital, and by inadequate facilities and insufficient manpower. As our colleges and universities set new enrollment records with the beginning of each new term, their financial needs have become the most stringent in their history. To continue their essential functions, much less to expand, our colleges require teaching and administrative staffs of the highest quality, but finding the means to pay salaries large enough to attract and keep such staffs has become a serious problem.

Hardest hit have been the private colleges which receive no tax support and are hard pressed by inflation and the decline in the purchasing power of the dollar because they have to depend largely on fixed incomes from their endowment funds. The private college must find more money for student scholarships and loans; more money for more teachers, even at present salary levels; money for maintaining present campuses; and more money for larger and better facilities—all this at a time when all our institutions of higher education are confronted with costs of operation that are spiraling upward. Tuition fees cover less than half the costs of maintenance of education in private colleges today, but if these schools were to charge students the full cost for their services they would price many highly qualified young people out of a college education.

Independent colleges and universities must therefore seek financial support from sources other than student fees. If funds do not come from private or corporate sources, there will be heavy pressure for support from public funds. If business does not quickly and intelligently shoulder more of this burden, government will have to. When government becomes the chief subsidizer of higher education, government controls will inevitably follow—at a much greater cost in many ways to the business community and to the nation.

We must make absolutely sure that higher education can continue to be free of political control, however well-intentioned such control is when it starts. Our colleges and universities must continue to maintain their historic position of liberty from the fetters of control by any political faction or by any force—from the right, the left, or the center.

In my strong and considered belief, therefore, corporate gifts to education must increase, and business must realize it has a special responsibility and a unique opportunity in the support of higher education—before it is too late—both for the advancement of the national good and for the more practical secondary purpose of making certain that its future supply of executives, scientists, researchers, supervisors, and labor force will be the best equipped in the world. Farsighted businessmen recognize the hard-headed good sense as well as the idealism of these facts. To them it is already apparent that there must be strong partnership between education and industry.

Many major business concerns have been providing aid to

the nation's universities and to individuals, thoughtfully and as a matter of considered long-range policy. But, in my opinion, business still has much farther to go in its support of higher education. Although a start has been made, few of us in business have been doing enough, in terms of what we can do; and unfortunately, some of us are doing nothing or dangerously little.

Twenty-five Cleveland business corporations have agreed that their companies will "make increases in corporate contributions commencing at once and increasing within three years to a minimum of not less than 1 per cent of income before taxes and thereafter gradually increasing as the need develops." The Council for Financial Aid to Education has said that the 1 per cent before taxes should be considered an ideal national goal for corporate giving to higher education, but it is not an exclusive device applicable to all corporations.

According to the Council, corporate giving to higher education is now about one third of 1 per cent of pretax earnings per year. If the national level of corporate support can be raised to the 1-per-cent goal, corporate support will climb from the present 150 million dollars to approximately 500 million a year, on the basis of present earnings.

I believe that more and more corporations will join in this worthy endeavor and that within the next decade corporate giving to higher education will attain the annual goal of 500 million dollars.

If our colleges and universities can be provided with the means to do their jobs well, the entire world will benefit, not merely the American business community. Financial contributions to the colleges and universities of the United States by the many individuals and corporations able to make them are really gilt-edged investments in a better and more secure future for all Americans.

As a businessman who has for many years worked for improved corporate support of education, I think I can offer a few practical suggestions to professional educators concerning the ways in which they can build a better case for corporate support.

1. I would attack the problem of more money for higher education somewhat as I would a problem in production and sales. Before any well-managed company undertakes the development of a new product (and often before changing an existing one), it surveys the consumer market thoroughly to make sure there is a widespread demand for the product. It also is well aware of what its competitors in the field are offering.

Why not, therefore, present higher education to corporations as a *product* and ask industry if it needs and wants this product? Of course it does. From where else are the skilled and trained personnel for the next decade—or the next generation—to come if not from our colleges and universities?

2. Educators can demonstrate to the prospective donors—all too easily, unfortunately—that their "plant expansion" *cannot be financed out of regular income*. And business, which must evaluate good investment against poor, can be shown how gilt-edged indeed is the security of their investment in education—and how tremendous is its growth potential.

3. Administrators, particularly college and university presidents, can convince business *why it should contribute more to the support of education*. Part of the duties of today's busy college president is the function of public relations executive for his institution and for his profession. He must spend a great deal of time and effort in showing the value of his institution to the businessmen of his community and to the representatives of national corporations. One way to do this, of course, is a consistent program whereby his institution participates widely and usefully in community affairs. As a result, businessmen will

usually be more willing to provide financial support if they see that they help the community and society when they increase their help to the college.

IN LINE WITH the foregoing suggestions to educators, I would like to examine briefly several others areas of American education on which improvements might be considered:

1. *Can we make better use of our present school facilities?* Couldn't college vacations and recesses be shortened, classes be offered on a full-day basis on Saturdays, and the variety of classes offered at night be increased?

If classes were conducted evenly throughout the day and into the evening, some professors and students might be inconvenienced by having to attend early-morning or late-afternoon classes, but this would be offset by having full utilization of the facilities. And there is nothing sacred about the summer holiday as such. It came into being here in the United States because ours was originally an agrarian economy where students were needed on the farms in the summer to raise and harvest the crops. Today, when agriculture is one of our most mechanized industries and when fewer than 10 per cent of our population live on farms, it would appear that the long summer vacation from school could be shortened.

There are some arguments against longer school terms. One of them is the fear that teachers would become overworked and no longer would have time for research and reflection so necessary to them if they are to teach well. But these problems can be solved. Classes throughout the year, or an extra semester or quarter, are not necessarily inconsistent with liberal vacations for teachers and reasonable teaching loads.

During periods of national emergency our institutions of higher education have instituted accelerated programs, making use of every physical and intellectual resource virtually around the clock.

We are faced with a national emergency now in education; we are lagging behind that part of the world we cannot describe as free. The extent of education in Soviet Russia and in China is becoming a greater challenge each year, especially in the sciences. Russian students today are not admitted to their universities unless they have completed five years of physics. They attend school six days a week, and from the sixth grade through what we call high school the typical Russian student works ten hours a day—six in class plus four hours of homework.

There is an ever-increasing contingent of young Americans who have the right and the qualifications to be educated, but whose numbers are already sorely taxing our existing educational resources. Can we not make better use of our educational time and facilities to accommodate them, *now*, until the necessary expansion can be accomplished?

An accelerated and longer school program, within reason, would also allow students training for medicine, engineering, the law, and other professions to embark on their active careers at an earlier age—and that much sooner be in a position to enrich the community and build their own lives.

Notable educators have pointed out in the recent past how lacking we are in programs for teaching the young mathematics, science, and foreign languages. It is high time we re-examine whether or not we are utilizing our present educational facilities at their maximum operational level.

2. *Are we beginning to overstress technology?* Education for Americans must do even more than offer more training in technology. We believe—and I think correctly—that the sciences and humanities must be taught concurrently, for science as such does not concern itself with questions of values or purpose or ethics. We must constantly be alert to keep a proper balance,

especially in these demanding times. The goal must be not merely to mass-produce first-rate technicians (and it cannot be merely to graduate "cultured" and genteel men and women) but to educate Americans whose technological skill is balanced with the understanding that enables them individually and as a nation to use their knowledge for the betterment of the world.

3. *What about foreign languages?* As the United States continues to play the leading role in world history destiny has thrust upon us and devotion to freedom demands, the educated American will require far more facility in foreign languages than he normally has now. Much of the success of Russia outside its own borders, for instance, has come because its representatives and emissaries are highly trained in the languages of the countries to which they are assigned and because they know in amazing depth the social customs and cultures of those countries.

Businessmen and diplomats have learned, to cite one example, how immensely helpful it is when our representatives who deal with our important neighbors in Central and South America are fluent in Spanish. As the economic and social integration of the Western democracies becomes more an actuality, our relationships with our Western European friends (with whom we must continue to cooperate closely) would indeed be strengthened if more of us were as adept in their languages as they are in ours.

In my opinion, such a unit as the Foreign Service Language School at Georgetown University is practically as important to our future security as are any of the government military academies. This is particularly true as we are faced with the difficult assignment of dealing—and dealing more successfully—with Russia and China. Many more Americans—in government, in the military, and in business—must understand and speak Russian and Chinese. A governmental academy the services of which are available to a wide student body would be a step in the right direction. I believe there should be a special government academy for the training of people for our Foreign Service. Such training would, of course, include languages and knowledge of customs and traditions of the various countries, with specialized study for those preferring assignment to a particular area.

4. *What about new educational methods and tools?* Particularly during the twentieth century, American education has had conflicting armchair theories and philosophies of education and has sometimes introduced new educational methods without adequate scientific preparation. Several distinguished educators have pointed out that this is because we have not conducted sufficient basic research on human learning and have not made much progress in ascertaining how best to develop the human intellect.

Now we cannot afford slapdash methods. We must make the maximum and the most efficient use of our educational manpower. Industry has been alert to innovations that can raise production per man-hour in its factories. The medical and engineering professions are likewise constantly doing research in the development of new processes, techniques, and media, all for the purpose of providing a better service with fewer man-hour resources.

But education is still suffering from the backwash of the warfare between the proponents of the misunderstood and misapplied "permissive" concepts of Freud and John Dewey and the strict disciplinarians in education.

We have long had gifted teachers. We are now in a position to apply technology and innovations to the tools which help them to reach the minds of more students.

The machine will never take the place of the good teacher, and nobody in his right mind would want to try. But with the aids of tape recordings, television, and aural-oral techniques in teaching languages (to name only a few available mechanical ones), the teacher can effectively reach a wider audience. The experimentation with educational television is a good example of the right approach.

The field of American education is still ripe for intelligent innovation.

IN THIS CHAPTER we have looked at education as the living, continuing process in which all of us become engaged in early childhood and from which we must continue to learn until we die. Since our future will be decided in inner space, "the space between the ears," we cannot let our education be otherwise.

The dilemma and opportunity for us and for education in our time, the change and the challenge, were summed up recently in a single sentence by the eminent anthropologist Margaret Mead:

"No one will live all his life in the world into which he was born, and no one will die in the world in which he worked in his maturity."

NINE

TRADE WITH THE REST OF THE WORLD

FOREIGN TRADE is one of those subjects practically every American has something to say about, unfortunately too often without full understanding. There are certain fundamentals too many of us are inclined to overlook in considering the foreign-trade policies that will be best for our country on a long-term basis.

Some people commit the error of thinking that foreign trade means only export. Actually, foreign trade—like all commerce —is a two-way street; seller and buyer generate an uninterrupted circular flow. With the proceeds of his sale, the seller is enabled to buy from his foreign customer; in turn, the foreign customer can once again buy from the home—in this case, American—seller. The full circle may involve two, three, four, or more countries, but no one country can go on only selling or just buying for a very long period of time.

Foreign trade is vital to the United States. In the kind of world we have today, it has political and military implications of great importance as well as commercial significance. Some of our allies have found it difficult to maintain their spending for necessary mutual defense without endangering their economies. For our own security and theirs, our free-world allies in Europe and the Far East must be strong, and one all-important way of strengthening their economies and potential defenses is our trade with them. If we were to stop trading with them, they would be forced to look elsewhere for markets and supplies.

Closely related to the need for trade to strengthen our allies is the sometimes-forgotten fact that we must have a healthy foreign trade if our own economy is to prosper and continue to grow rapidly. Buying from and selling to other nations helps raise our own standard of living. We could perhaps be economically self-sufficient for a time, but we would not be as well off as we could be, and in the long run our economy would be weakened. Freer international trade is therefore essential to the prosperity of the United States and the security of the entire free world.

Foreign trade gives us an opportunity to specialize and gives other countries the same opportunity. The gains of this international and domestic specialization were first spelled out, and never better spelled out, than by Adam Smith in his *Wealth of Nations,* published in 1776. Specialization permits greater size of markets. This, for example, is of enormous gain to Canada, as it is to many United States industries. It permits taking advantage of varying geographical resources.

The argument I like best is that foreign trade makes better jobs. It does not so much make more jobs, it just makes better jobs. *Better jobs* is a simple way of saying that we thereby advance our productivity and total output.

FEW OF OUR CITIZENS today fail to recognize the need for political and social cooperation with other nations, but a good many of them distrust enlarging international economic cooperation. Many Americans are now asking such questions as: Will we not depress our industry at home if we buy abroad? Since American labor can produce the things Americans need, why pay foreigners to do it? Why should we sacrifice our own prosperity in a futile quest for foreign good will?

The facts of today's life provide ample and clear answers to these questions. Even the opponents of foreign trade must agree that we want to expand the sale of products from our most efficient high-productivity industries—which provide high-wage jobs for our workers. Enlarged foreign sales or exports can help do this. We also need to sell more of our agricultural products, particularly surpluses. Our agriculture is exceedingly efficient, and more food exports can help farmers prosper. Exports thus can help enlarge the markets for our highly efficient industries, create jobs, and raise incomes in these industries.

Economist Peter Drucker emphasized the importance of foreign trade when he pointed out: "Every tenth American gets his paycheck from an export sale; every fourth depends on imported raw materials." And we should not forget the importance of foreign trade to our shipping industry and to the maintenance of our Merchant Marine, which is also a part of our own arsenal of defense.

The one positive certainty about our foreign trade is that other countries will buy from us only so long as they are selling to us. We can export only if we import—and one good way to cultivate friendship and good will in other nations is to buy their products. Thus, from any sound economic point of view, today we must buy abroad if we are to sell our own goods abroad; only if we import is the profitable export of a wide diversity of American-made products possible.

Moreover, we gain much by our purchases abroad. Our imports include large quantities of raw materials we either do not have or produce in insufficient quantity for our needs. Among them are paper and wood pulp, sugar and coffee, diamonds for industry and jewelry, copra, silk, spices, furs, jute, tin, and many others. We also buy many finished products that are produced either uniquely or more efficiently abroad, such as Swiss watches, French and German wines, Paris gowns, Italian lace, cheeses, English textiles, and so on. These consumer goods in turn help enrich our American standard of living.

When international trade is moving along in all directions at a lively clip, the dollars we pay for imports return quickly to us as payment for our exports. The rate of turnover and the volume of trade is a measure of economic welfare on a world-wide scale. Every time our dollars round the circuit they signal another completed transaction that has benefited all parties concerned. With every turnover of dollars—whether among Americans themselves or between America and other nations—there is a gain for all.

GREAT COMMERCIAL NATIONS DO NOT become second- or third-rate economic powers in one single catastrophic collapse. A nation tends to decline slowly, and decline begins when competition ends. Competition is the lifeblood of industrial strength and efficiency. When a country increases tariff protection to reduce the "stress" of competition from other countries, its own economy begins to weaken, to lose efficiency and strength. Among the other nations in our era that have unwisely sought escape from competition was France, which took little capsules of protection from 1936 to 1956 and thereby greatly weakened itself. We must learn from others and not take the same path of protectionism toward decline.

France is indeed a striking example of how to grow weak in two decades. Among other things, France followed highly restrictive foreign-trade policies and instituted many protective devices, much as some labor and business managements in the United States are seeking protection today.

Did this protection and sheltering of French industries from world competition make France strong? Far from it. The result was to make France weak and ineffectual both in production and in trade.

General de Gaulle recognized this fact upon his accession to power in France a few years ago. He abandoned the protective policies. He exposed the French economy to world competition.

What has been the result? A very strong French productive economy, with a rising standard of living, strong monetary reserves, a strong franc.

Those of our industries that feel impelled to ask special protection through tariffs should state their cases honestly, and just as honestly accept the verdict. Ours is a free-enterprise system, which means that it is a profit-and-loss system. The industry which still leans upon protectionism for itself must accept society's ultimate verdict that if it cannot survive without protection in these prosperous times, it must shift over to lines in which it *can* survive. In the face of the present world struggle we cannot afford chronically weak and inefficient spots in our economy year after year.

Postwar developments in Germany contain an important lesson for the United States concerning foreign trade policies and demonstrate why protectionism is unwise. West Germany, defeated and destroyed in World War II, has now accumulated large gold and monetary reserves. Germany now also enjoys one of the strongest currencies in Europe because it has followed the path of free enterprise since 1945. It has rebuilt a strong and competitive industry. West Germany has moved toward free international trade more and more. Putting her industry in a competitive position has made it both efficient and highly productive.

IN THE UNITED STATES, our own situation with respect to foreign trade has changed considerably since World War II. Immediately after the war we had no export problem, no difficulty selling our goods abroad; we were the only large-scale producer left in the world. The great European industrial economies lay prostrate. Our exports were limited only by the availability of dollars in other countries.

This increase in our exports immediately following the war revealed two important things: (1) Our exports helped propel our economy to increasingly high levels. (2) Our exports were paid for largely by lending abroad, or, more important, by foreign aid—in other words, simply giving the exports away. Foreign aid under the Marshall Plan, through which Western Europe was rehabilitated, helped greatly to finance our own exports shortly after 1945.

By the middle 1950s the other industrial nations of the free world had made great economic recovery, and we began to run into vigorous competition from both Europe and Japan. Today, some of these countries have production costs far lower than ours in many lines. Others of our allies may not yet have appreciably lower production costs, but they are striving for advantage and are working day and night to increase their export sales. This rising tide of new competition forces us in the United States to put greater attention to and emphasis on our own costs and efficiency and on the enlargement of our export sales picture.

Prices, wages, and costs are crucial factors in the growing world competition we face in the years directly ahead. While it would appear that the rate of inflation in the United States has been arrested, we must continue to combat rising prices and costs. Sharper competition from abroad now makes thoroughly clear to us that cost and price increases of American goods cannot exceed those of competing nations in international markets if we are to retain and enlarge our share of the free world's trade.

Consumer research abroad or foreign market development should not be confined only to foreign countries; it must start at the point of production in our own country. We need to inspect our standards for goods for our foreign customers, and we should build up an American reputation for shipping quality products to foreign buyers. In many cases product designs must be especially adapted and marketing methods changed. Our transportation facilities—particularly our ports—should be inspected to insure that our products can and will be efficiently transported. To increase our foreign markets, we should make it easier for our foreign customers to purchase our products. We should cater to them by giving our foreign buyers the products they want, not necessarily the products we would like them to buy.

Corporations in the United States are not only reorganizing themselves to meet the changing conditions in their domestic and foreign markets; they are also seeking to establish themselves in the world market place by either setting up in foreign countries plants of their own or making acceptable tie-ups with established foreign manufacturers. Many companies are vigorously developing their markets by working out cooperative business arrangements abroad which permit them to use their American "know-how" at the same time they reduce their amount of American investment.

CONSIDERING THE FAR EAST, the most important postwar trade problem arises from the precarious position in which our ally Japan finds herself. One of the major policy objectives of the United States in the Pacific is the promotion of a stable and democratic Japan. We wish to see Japan strong, capable of defending herself, and willing to contribute to the common defense of freedom in the area.

The first requirement of a stable free society—and this certainly holds true for present-day Japan—is a vital and dynamic economy, productive enough to furnish the people an adequate standard of living and capable of supporting the necessary defense forces. Japan can maintain her economic balance today only by trading with other countries. And our friendship will grow, our alliance with Japan will be strengthened only if the United States is willing to engage in a considerable amount of two-way trade with Japan.

Japan lost many of her previous rich sources of raw materials as a result of World War II—Manchuria, Formosa, Korea, and Sakhalin. When the Communists closed the door to mainland China, Japan lost a major natural market and a traditional source of food and raw material. On top of this, the population of Japan has increased tremendously. Japan's need and desire to import from the United States—especially food products and raw materials—has become more acute as a result of this combination of circumstances.

Ever since the war, Japan's serious deficit in foreign trade has been met by the United States in the form of one type of aid or another. American spending in the form of special military procurement and the personal expenditures of our troops and civilians in Japan—millions of dollars each year—has helped Japan finance her necessary imports from us and add to her dollar reserves. Japan is using these dollars to buy our goods, and will continue to do so: she needs to buy from us and we want to sell to her. But to buy from us, Japan must also sell to us: we must import more from Japan. The only alternative would be to enlarge our foreign aid to Japan, not a good choice for either nation. And if we bar Japanese products through higher tariffs we only make it necessary to advance more funds to Japan to keep her economy sound. The only realistic long-run solution is trade, not aid—and Japan much prefers trade.

What can be done to reduce this continuing burden on the United States? In the long run, Japan must be able to expand its exports. The greatest potential markets for Japan are in South and Southeast Asia. If this area were today not either held by the Communists or economically sick or underdeveloped we could, as in the past, buy raw materials—more from them than we sell to them—and furnish Asia with dollar credits. Japan could gain in turn, by selling to these South Asian countries, the dollars with which to pay for its own purchases from the United States. As always must happen, the benefits would spread in a free-flowing, multilateral trade cycle. For this to work in the future as a solution to Japan's problem (and consequently part of the world's problems), communism must be stopped in Southeast Asia, and we must direct our efforts toward developing the underdeveloped nations there.

We need not only to lower our existing tariffs against Japanese goods; we should also continue to assist Japan in her efforts to obtain reductions in the discriminatory tariffs and quotas placed against her products by many other countries of the free world, particularly in Europe. Success in this area would help strengthen the free world as a whole and would result in some sharing by other nations of the responsibility for keeping the Japanese economy strong. Furthermore, as the underdeveloped nations are able to enlarge their industries, with a resultant increase in the production of manufactured goods, both Europe and the United States should share in accepting such products of so-called cheap labor. To exclude them through restrictive and arbitrary measures would discourage the economic development of those countries and impose additional artificial barriers to improvement of conditions on a world-wide scale. It would also keep "cheap labor" from approaching the labor level, and therefore the cost-to-produce level, of the highly developed countries.

ALL TRADE ENHANCES WELFARE. Individuals or business concerns exchange their products only because each gains by so doing. Both theory and experience have shown that when each individual specializes in what he can do best, and exchanges his products with other specialists in other fields, all benefit and the total supply of goods available for consumption is greatly increased. If each American family today were compelled to produce everything it consumed, for instance, the nation would rapidly return to an earlier level of a bare subsistence.

Our standard of living has become high because individuals and firms specialize in producing articles to exchange with each other. The application of this immutable law of specialization cannot now stop at the boundaries of any one country, if in fact it ever has during recorded history. Therefore, specialization and trade benefit nations in much the same way they do individuals. Restrictions on trade are economically unsound and costly. Economic nationalism is expensive to any country that indulges in it—and, because of the unquestionable validity and success of free trade, the burden of proof must fall on those who would destroy it.

When we import goods that other nations can produce better or less expensively than we can, we enable Americans to concentrate on those lines that *we* can produce more efficiently and cheaply. An excellent example is the gunny sack, that cheap and durable wrapping so important for handling a wide variety of products. It is made of burlap, a fabric woven from jute, which is grown almost entirely in India and Pakistan. Production of burlap requires an appropriate climate, much labor, and very little machinery. These Asian countries in which jute is a major crop are best equipped and endowed to produce burlap—and so we import it from them. If we did not buy burlap from India and Pakistan, we might substitute American-made cotton sacks. But they would serve most uses no better (for some they would be less satisfactory) and they would cost a great deal more. Thus we gain from the present pattern of burlap trade.

A tiny amount of our machinery-reinforced labor pays for a great deal of burlap from India and Pakistan. We pay high wages at home and get low-cost material for sacks from abroad. In exchange for their burlap, India and Pakistan get from us machinery that will help them produce more and attain a higher standard of living for their workers. Thus India and Pakistan also gain from the present pattern of burlap trade.

It has been estimated that the goods we normally export to Southeast Asia are produced by no more than two hundred thousand American workers and that the goods we normally get back from that region are produced by about twenty million workers. This emphasizes once again (among other things) the value to our labor force of American industry's big-machinery investment in each worker. The trade with "cheap-labor" countries is truly an advantageous exchange for us. And the low-wage countries which usually supply us with raw materials also benefit: the workers in these poorer countries are thus provided jobs and incomes and with the dollars to buy some of the things made in the United States.

International trade is necessary to our own agricultural and industrial health, too. In agriculture, we have been exporting from 20 to 40 per cent of our annual output of cotton, rice, wheat, soybeans, sorghum, tobacco, tallow, and lard. Our exports of industrial product include rolling-mill machinery, textile machinery, printing machinery, oil-field equipment, office appliances, motor trucks, and agricultural machinery, to mention only a few.

Without exports we cannot support our at-times excess industrial capacity, the potential that could be turned immediately into full-scale defense production should the need come. This fact and many others make it very plain that we are not self-sufficient and dare not try to withdraw again into the never-never land of isolationism. We are now moreover in the position of world leadership. We cannot escape the implications of that position—which include a liberal trade policy.

So THE QUESTION NOW IS: How can we develop more trade? What can the United States import in larger amounts without significant harm to the American farmer, American industry, or the American worker? Remember in answering that as our imports increase so will our exports. Imports will beget exports, not only of the important industrial products which help keep wages high but also of the agricultural products which help keep farm income high.

Higher incomes for farmers and for workers in the export industries will enable them to buy and consume more domestically produced goods and use domestic services as well as those that are imported; thus expansion will come in still other domestic industries. Many of the imported items will be different from any we produce at home. Others will be much less expensive than similar articles now available. These cheaper competing goods may, it is true, injure a few American firms, at least temporarily. But American consumers will benefit from the lower prices—and we are all consumers. It appears quite clear that we can increase considerably our imports of foreign-made goods with great benefit to the vast majority of Americans. Even the competition, which could seem superficially painful to a very few, could bring out the best in them—to our benefit—in the long run.

It would certainly be to our national advantage to import more of certain minerals of which our own supplies are limited (magnesium, for instance, and tungsten and vanadium). It would also be advantageous to import more goods than we now do that require types of craftsmanship not developed in this country (handmade lace and linens, wearing apparel, china, and art objects among them). More imports of such products would bring pleasure to all of us, especially when we realize that our purchases of more of them make it possible for our farmers to sell more wheat and tobacco and cotton and peanuts as well as help our friends in other lands. The volume of these imported articles is and will remain relatively insignificant in our huge

American market. But to the smaller countries that produce such goods, an increase in volume that would be small by our standards would often be large enough significantly to improve their economic status.

Americans today are probably the world's greatest travelers. Travel in foreign countries has the same economic and financial effect as importing goods from abroad. The dollars American tourists spend abroad are the same dollars American importers pay for foreign goods. They make it possible for people abroad to buy more products of American farms and factories. When we pay *anyone* a dollar, the only place that dollar can ultimately be spent is in the United States.

Since it is almost certain that productivity in this country will increase in the future, it is almost certain also that American incomes will grow in the future. Such growth will be a measure of our economic progress. Let us then plan to use more of this growing income to enlarge our sensible consumption—to enrich our own lives and the lives of those economically less fortunate by utilizing the multitude of low-cost-to-produce goods that can be brought here from all over the world.

And in this connection we should remember once again that world trade is based on multilateral exchange. It is not necessarily restricted to two-way, direct exchange between only two countries. We do not always have to buy from the same country to which we sell. The dollar volume of our exports to the Far East exceeds considerably the value of our imports from that area. But the dollars we pay for imports from the Far East flow to Europe, to pay for products manufactured there. Europeans then use the same dollars to buy from the United States— chiefly food products, of which the United States now produces a surplus and of which Europe does not currently produce enough for its own needs. This process is called *triangular trade*, the three points of the triangle being the United States, the Far

East, and Europe. When many countries are involved, the usual term is *multilateral trade*.

ANOTHER IMPORTANT TERM in the vocabulary of trade with the rest of the world is *reciprocal trade*. Reciprocity based on mutual agreement for removal of trade restrictions between nations has long been recognized by our government as healthy and helpful to foreign trade. Before World War II, the United States had negotiated bilateral trade agreements with twenty-nine countries.

Today it is clearly necessary that there be even wider trade arrangements among many nations. To that end the General Agreement on Tariffs and Trade was negotiated in 1947, providing for a multilateral approach to the solution of international trade problems, with primary attention given to the reduction of trade barriers. Essentially, the Agreement schedules the products on which tariffs are reduced or "bound" against increase, with separate schedules for each country. It also provides a code under which the import and export transactions of the signatory nations are conducted.

More than thirty countries, whose economies account for some 80 per cent of present world trade, participate in GATT. This is for the benefit of both ourselves and the free world. We should fight to the limit any claims from any quarter that we cannot afford such trade-agreement programs in a period such as the present. In our world we can afford less than ever before *not* to join in reciprocal trade agreements.

In these uncertain but challenging times so marked with difficulties in securing peace in the world, the free nations would do well to bear in mind Benjamin Franklin's admonition to the American colonies that if they did not hang together they would very likely hang separately. The United States today does not have the margin of strength that will allow it to be indifferent to the needs of its friends. We must strengthen and enlarge all trade and economic bonds that may bind us together more firmly. History teaches us that trade has always been the life-blood of our own states, of regional organisms, and of inter-continental empires. And without any doubt, free trade will remain the bloodstream of any successful federation of free peoples in the future.

Thus our foreign trade program is crucial. It has properly been realized to be a cornerstone in our foreign policy. A free trade policy is inescapable evidence that we intend to work, devotedly and completely, with our allies to develop mutual well-being. Nobody and no nation today can "go it alone"; our allies cannot prosper without us, nor we in the final analysis without them. The welfare of the United States is inseparable from the welfare of other nations. No nation is any longer sufficient unto itself.

WITH RESPECT TO United States policy toward economic integration abroad, the historic policy of the United States has been to encourage economic unions everywhere. One of the first tests came in a proposed prewar Danubian federation or customs union to replace that which had existed in the days of the Austro-Hungarian Empire. Lowering tariffs by these countries reciprocally for the members of the group only would run against the "most-favored-nation" clauses in our commercial treaties with these Danubian countries; however, we were willing to forego our rights. We took this position on the ground that if they could by such arrangements improve the internal prosperity of the group, the United States would gain.

We would gain because as they became more prosperous their total trade with us would grow. We trade by far the most with prosperous countries and by far the least with unprosperous countries. Our trade with the unprosperous Balkan countries was extremely small. If they could unite economically and become more prosperous, having thereby created a larger market area, they would be the gainers and so would we.

It is this general view that has led us persistently to encourage economic union in Europe. While we would like to see a United States of Europe, an economic union there would help greatly to enlarge our trade with Europe, not diminish it. We would gain stronger allies. Settling some of the economic issues in an economic union in Europe would lead them to establish a political union, and thus the final integrated gain would be secured.

The European Common Market is proceeding from its initial birth in the Treaty of Rome of March 11, 1957. The group, sometimes referred to as the "Inner Six," consists of West Germany, France, Italy, Belgium, Luxembourg, and Holland. The "Outer Seven" (now Eight) include the adjacent countries, heavily under the leadership of Britain, mistakenly unwilling to join with the Common Market group but continuously flirting with it.

The Common Market group has already added to the welfare and current prosperity of most of its members. The economic recovery, especially in Germany and France, has been very strong and is continuing. The formation of the Common Market results in much larger additional capital investment programs; these give prosperity in today's activity and promise a much stronger economic base for tomorrow.

The United States policy should further encourage the union of the present two European groups. It will come, and we hope soon.

Western Hemisphere economic integration has far less significance, desirable as would be its political meaning. With Canada, we are the finished goods producer. The Latin American countries are raw material producers. They buy from us to the extent of their dollar resources, and do not have tariffs for normal "protection" purposes but for revenue purposes and to restrain buying to equality with the available supplies of dollars. We generally do not have tariffs against their production of bananas, pineapples, coffee, or timber, for example. To start with, our trade with these countries is complementary; in Europe, in contrast, it has been competitive. Union there will create a sizable market and sizable industries. Europe needs both.

TODAY'S MANY DEMANDS FOR tariffs to protect us in our production against foreign competition, especially that from low-wage countries, must be resisted. As a country, we are not going to be put out of business by low-wage competition; there have always been such low wages elsewhere and our foreign trade has grown. If we yield to the clamor, we will be sending the United States into economic decline.

Of course other countries can produce some things better than we. And it is just as true the other way around. We have to produce on a large scale with the aid of much capital. Others have to concentrate low-wage labor into their products. Some illustrations will make this clear. In the South Canton province of China before the war, an entire family's production of rice, even at two crops a year, was about 268 bushels. We can produce 10,000 bushels per rice grower, using machinery, combines, and tractors. If our wages are twenty dollars a day, we obtain a production that is almost forty times Chinese production. We can pay wages twenty-five times as high per man and yet have a balance for the rent of machinery. And we have sold rice abroad in other countries against their cheap labor rates; flat land, irrigation ditches, dams made with machinery, and the tractor, combine, and seeder make this possible.

The same is true in coal. We have carried coals to Newcastle and Germany. Our wages are now $23.50 a day and our per-man production twelve tons. The cost of labor to mine a ton of our coal is two dollars. In contrast, in Germany and Britain the day's wages for a coal miner is about eight dollars and a half. The amount of coal mined is about a ton and one third. The labor cost there is about $6.25 per ton, three times our labor cost per ton of coal mined. In other words, our labor cost is much lower than theirs, and the productivity of our miners is about seven times as great. Many other examples could be given.

If we did not make the adjustments which are required by those of our industries which cannot meet foreign competition, but preserved these industries without change, we would be making America poor. By making the adjustments, we make America effective and rich in its total production and standard of living. Businessmen who profess enterprise should not ask the federal government to make goods more expensive for workers and the average citizen. That is what some of their tariff proposals today would do.

TEN

AID AND A FREE WORLD

TRADE AND AID have a similar sound, but they are not spelled alike and they do not operate alike. Both are helpful—and necessary—in the world and the age in which we live. They are, in fact, sometimes confused with one another in the thinking of some Americans, perhaps because in the recent past they have been interacting forces. In Chapter 9 we took a look at some of the issues involved in foreign trade; now let us examine, at least in general terms, what might be considered its cousin—foreign aid.

We Americans have the most effective political, social and economic system ever enjoyed by man. Elsewhere throughout the world, the peoples of many less fortunate countries still aspire to political freedom as all-embracing, to economic opportunity as broad, and to institutions as responsible as those we enjoy and too often accept as a matter of course.

In the present ideological struggle between East and West, many of these underdeveloped countries are uncommitted to either major side and uncertain what course to take for themselves. A great many, perhaps all, of them look to the United States for leadership and help in finding their own right direction. At the same time, they are being bombarded incessantly with propaganda designed to turn them toward a Communist "solution" of their problems. If we ignore the predicament of the less fortunate countries we will force them into the Communist bloc.

We must accept the fact that we do not live alone in the world, as individuals or as a nation—nor could we now live alone if we wanted to. As we noted elsewhere in another connection, prosperity and material success carry with them certain responsibilities. It is not enough merely for free enterprise to prosper in the United States. Even if there were no clear and present danger to our way of life posed by the fanatic adherents of another kind of political system, we could not long afford to permit countless millions of human beings to remain engulfed in poverty and misery. Since the danger does exist, we must not let hungry people and illiterate youth believe that their only hope is to turn to communism. The strong possibility that underdeveloped and newly independent nations could become Soviet satellites is more than sufficient reason for continuing our program of international cooperation and foreign aid. This is a grim reality that cannot be ignored even by those who would oppose foreign aid. It is in the national interest of the United States to assist in speeding up the development of the poorer nations and to help these countries help themselves.

What has happened in Cuba has awakened us to the fact that the welfare of other countries must be aided or we lose our own welfare and safety. All of Latin America with its vast resources and population has had almost no development comparable to our own. Yet the area is not overpopulated; it is not poor in resources. Its educational progress is minute. We want Latin America to be committed on our side. This means we must follow through aggressively and do everything we can with our aid and our technicians to assist the Latin American countries to make substantial progress.

Between 1913 and 1960 the United States extended foreign aid in one form or another worth about 120 billion dollars in goods and services. From the end of the second world war to 1960 we gave to non-Americans grants or loans totaling more than fifty billion dollars. While we may have received little if any measurable, tangible benefit in return, unprejudiced men recognize that we have gained. We have kept much of the world safe for democracy; Fascism and Nazism have been destroyed as state systems in operation, and so far many nations have been saved from the Communist advance. The very fact that our way of life has survived the terrible onslaughts of the fifty years just past is gain indeed. And survival is at least part-proof that our dollars of foreign aid extended in the past have been far from wasted.

Furthermore, by supplying aid to other countries in the past we have enlarged our own national capacity to produce. As a result of the attendant high employment and high wages in our country, we have also increased our power to consume. The loss of production during the Great Depression of the 1930s was much more costly to us than *all* our expenditures for foreign aid during the last fifty years. And since World War II we have been able to extend billions of dollars in aid to the rest of the world while, at the same time, continuing to raise to record high levels our standard of living at home.

Over the years our foreign economic aid has averaged less than 2 per cent of our national income. The total amount appropriated for 1961—less than four billion dollars, of which almost half is for military assistance—does not amount to even 1 per cent of the highest national income in the world. Surely we could afford to double or triple our foreign aid for the sake of our own security and for world stability. It would be a small enough price to pay.

So FAR AS the Communist economic offensive is concerned at present, there has been a significant shift in the global strategy of communism. Soviet Russia, having built up its military strength and technology, now realizes—as do we—that a nuclear war would be mutually suicidal. However, having built up her industrial machine and having made great economic progress, Russia is now able to use her new economic power to further her political aims abroad (which have *not* changed) without resorting to nuclear warfare. The Communists intend to use their rising economic power to achieve their objective of world domination.

I believe that every citizen of the free world should be grateful for this change. We should welcome the shift of the struggle to the economic front, where production and distribution of goods rather than the destruction of lives will be decisive factors. But we must continue to evaluate this new Soviet-Chinese challenge with the same urgency used to judge the threats of missiles and the hydrogen bomb. We cannot go back comfortably to sleep. The Communist purpose has not changed; only the means for achieving that purpose may have been shifted.

It would be suicide for us to underestimate the economic potential and the political strategy of the Communists. Theirs is a tough, fully calculated economic assault. They are playing this game for keeps, and they have absolutely no scruples about the techniques they use. In the Communist rule book, the end—world domination—justifies any means. We have a long, hard struggle ahead of us. We shall have to keep up our own fight at every level in all walks of life, with all our might and determination. Important as the military struggles in Korea and Indochina and the war of nerves over Berlin have been, the less newsworthy economic conflict will be no less important and will probably be much more decisive over a long period.

The Soviet bloc began extending foreign aid to uncommitted and underdeveloped countries in 1954 and has been intensifying the program ever since. By mid-1960 the U.S.S.R. had extended more than four billion dollars in gifts and credits. The *amount* of aid given by the Communist bloc is considerably less than the amount given by the United States. But because of their highly effective administration and propaganda, the Communists are achieving a political and psychological impact in the world far out of proportion to the fiscal amount of their aid. With us, unfortunately, the opposite is the case.

We should applaud Moscow's bona-fide, no-strings-attached grants and loans to underdeveloped countries. Russia has a significant industrial power and thus a humanitarian duty to assist poorer countries, nonpolitically. Russia should therefore be willing to give assistance through the United Nations if she truly has a desire to minister to the material needs of the poorer countries. Unfortunately Moscow, and more recently Peking also, uses foreign aid to penetrate and infiltrate a few countries carefully selected for their potential value in the Communist plan of political conquest. Communist foreign aid has already achieved some successes. It has weakened too many of the traditional friendships between the United States and peoples in Asia, Africa, and even in South and Central America. And Soviet trade agreements with such countries as Burma, Iceland, Egypt, and Iraq, as well as incursions in Ghana and Cuba, are resulting in new political alignments which are disturbing.

As part of its foreign-aid strategy, the Communist bloc is rapidly stepping up its program of technical assistance. Although they entered this field only recently, by mid-1960 some 6800 Communist technicians—including 1100 military advisers —were working in twenty-three countries outside the Communist area. The United States, which has been engaged in technical assistance much longer, had only 5800 economic and 950 military technicians abroad in 1960.

The essential purposes of Communist foreign economic aid remain political and psychological. Their technical experts sent to uncommitted nations always include "political scientists" trained in the techniques of organizing riots and revolution, men intensely dedicated to communism. From their own statements, it is obvious that the Soviets and their allies intend to destroy the governments now in power in these underdeveloped nations. They intend to spread their economic influence so that carefully selected countries can first be made dependent upon Soviet assistance and then can be controlled by Soviet methods —all this without any need at all to fight a nuclear war. The Communists are now giving high priority to this program among the uncommitted peoples of Asia and the Middle East, the new nations of Africa, and even our free neighbors in Latin America.

The Politburo's program is not based on the profit motive or on good business principles in the American sense. The Communists strike hard trade bargains where they can—but where there is poverty and economic exploitation is impossible at once, they may give superficially favorable trade bargains and proffer substantial aid. In every case, however, they strike hard political bargains: the price is freedom. The Communists are not concerned with economic profit for themselves or with wages or fringe benefits for the workers. Freedom of the individual is of no consequence in their system. The Soviets are perfectly willing, when necessary, to incur financial loss to themselves for a sufficiently large political gain.

Soviet tactics are unquestionably deceptive and full of political guile. Add to this the fact that Soviet Russia is a growing economic power, our number-one rival in the world. The result is frightening—and it should be. The outcome of this fierce trade-and-aid competition, ultimately for the hearts and minds of mankind as well as for the markets of the underdeveloped countries, will certainly have a forceful effect on our welfare in the United States. American businessmen, who operate with normal business methods within limits established by the profit criteria of private business, cannot possibly counter the Soviet challenge individually. We can stop the economic march of the

Communists only through well-advised, organized group action sanctioned by the government and through foreign aid supplied by the government.

Communist China is a rising economic power also not to be overlooked in our present struggle. Red China has already made grants to Cambodia, Ceylon, and Nepal, and is participating more and more fully in the aid program of the Communist bloc. We can expect Communist China to attempt to enlarge its role in both aid and trade in the years ahead.

THE AMERICAN COUNTEROFFENSIVE must develop action on at least three levels if we are to cope successfully with the Communist offensive. First, we must maintain military defenses so strong that the Communists will be literally afraid to attack us with missiles, hydrogen bombs, or conventional methods of warfare for fear of massive retaliation. Second, we must expand our production so greatly that we can support a rising standard of living for our own people while we maintain our defenses. Third, our economy must also generate enlarged amounts of foreign aid to stop the Communist economic offensive where it stands. We must have the courage and old-fashioned American gumption to carry the benefits of our system to the less fortunate in the world through aid, loans, and trade. Our Mutual Security Program, the United Nations, private programs, and perhaps other programs not yet effected can be the vehicles for helping those countries now threatened—often more seriously than they realize—by the lengthening Red shadow.

I am unswervingly convinced that, if the American system is to survive the Communist onslaught, we must enter this newest and grimmest economic competition with the same determination and creative imagination that was used to plan and build our great nation. We must firmly commit ourselves *as a nation* to help other nations with dollars, ideas, and skills. Our technicians and business enterprises could and should shift some of their attention from the domestic scene to the Far East, the Middle East, South America, and the other areas in which there is need and desire for progress. We must cooperate with and support all government programs designed to stop the Communist advance.

A nation, like an individual, does not know how much it can do until it tries. There is little doubt that the United States has accomplished more in total production because it has tried more, far more than it had expected, in providing foreign aid. This foreign aid leads to enlarging our exports. Larger exports are an important sinew in national strength. As I have said before, we must increase our exports and expand our foreign trade.

If we must make a choice between exporting more, even if we grant loans and aid, and importing more and not making loans and granting aid, let us keep up our export power. Then if war or a national emergency arises, we have that power in reserve for our own welfare. If the rest of the world should be cut off from us, we would then not have to export and the resources we formerly used in export would be released for other domestic purposes. In contrast, a country importing more would, in case of a like emergency, be cut off from imports. It would then have to take resources from other national purposes to develop substitute production for the lost imports. Thus we see that an export excess gives elements of strength and import dependence creates elements of weakness. Let the United States keep maximum strength. Exports assist to this end.

A really intelligent understanding of the Communist threat can furnish the dynamic force needed to blast a way to national unity in our fight against the Sino-Soviet economic and political offensive. Recognition of this grave danger must dissolve opposition from isolationist groups. We must search for better understanding of the less developed nations, of their ancient religions and cultures—which are admittedly sometimes difficult for Americans to comprehend or to appreciate. Full recognition of the threat of communism will also assure that American industrial interests face up to the need for expanded foreign aid, even though their narrower self-interests may suffer a bit when more aid is extended. Indeed, the fear of communism in and of itself should be sufficient cause for all Americans to unite and take the offensive against it. We must not hold back because we think that transferring an additional small amount of our great wealth will ruin our economy, because it will not. We must not let our good fortune of comfortable living make us complacent and stifle our good will toward sharing our wealth with less fortunate individuals in poorer countries.

ONE OF THE REASONS "foreign aid" is a scare phrase to some people today is the result of a misunderstanding—some of these people think that aid means giveaway, pure and simple. Not so. American foreign aid has many facets, and we shall spend most of the rest of this chapter looking at the major ones—foreign investment, multilateral aid, direct aid.

First: foreign investment and American know-how. Between 1883 and 1913 the countries of Western Europe (Britain, France, Belgium, Holland, and Germany) invested a total of forty billion dollars in the rest of the world. During that time the United States received about half these loans—a colossal amount compared to the incomes of the countries which put up the money. And every American now lives better because our fathers and grandfathers had the use of this capital which helped them build our great industry. Today the shoe is on the other foot; we are now in a position to lend our money and our skills to help underdeveloped nations abroad.

As a positive and coherent part of our economic offensive for freedom, American business must do everything possible to export capital, administrative know-how, and technical skills to the newly developing areas. If we will help build plants in the underdeveloped countries, the products of such plants will reflect local labor costs and therefore can be offered at attractive prices on the local market. Simultaneously, the plants will create jobs and raise local purchasing power. By putting our funds and our management skill to work in the less developed nations, we can develop profitable enterprises and gradually create new markets for ourselves. And by our example we can also stimulate other businesses in these countries.

Such a program of lending capital and skill can grow in importance if American businessmen will become more familiar with the significant areas of Asia and Africa in which our trade efforts and investment have been small. Up to 1960, all of Africa, all of the Middle East, and all of Asia including Japan have received less than 15 per cent of our total overseas private investment. These are precisely the areas in which the Communist bloc is concentrating most of its efforts.

As private business begins constructively to enter the various areas of particular concern to American foreign policy, it seems appropriate enough that the government reward and encourage such investments through tax concessions or other devices. Through our Mutual Security Program our government is advising and assisting underdeveloped countries in the establishment of institutions and programs that will provide a favorable climate for private investment. American industry can help materially in this. A number of the underdeveloped countries have entered into agreements which provide private investors guarantees against specific risks of expropriation and currency inconvertibility. Further consideration needs to be given to treaties leading to the elimination of double taxation of money earned abroad—earnings that are taxed both by the foreign country and by the United States. Such policies would help encourage a much more rapid flow abroad of American lending.

Second: multilateral aid. After World War II, as the United States sought to supply the most urgent needs of the devastated countries—victors and vanquished alike—we developed the Marshall Plan to speed Europe's economic recovery. It worked well. Europe has now recovered to a point at which it can and must assume a fair share of the burden of economic assistance to the less developed nations.

Although we still contribute by far the largest share, the United States does not bear the entire burden of extending aid to the less developed regions of the world. The United Kingdom is increasing its assistance yearly. In relation to its size, Canada's aid in the Colombo Plan and through the agencies of the United Nations is considerable. West Germany has been making significant contributions to Greece, Turkey, India, Israel, and the United Arab Republic. France contributes to the development of its former overseas territories, now independent African nations but still members of the French Community. Japan pays substantial reparations to the Philippines, Indonesia, Vietnam, and Burma; Japan is also assisting Brazil, Cambodia, and Laos. The European Economic Community is establishing an "overseas fund" to finance economic and social development in overseas territories of its member countries.

Although the flow of aid from throughout the free world is increasing, the need for assistance is growing still faster in the newly independent countries. To meet this need, the more fortunate nations must share the burden to the limit of their abilities. The United States cannot do the job alone, nor should it be expected to. The loss of gold by the United States has given us an indicator readily suggesting to all allied nations the need for their joining in foreign-aid programs, and that is going to lighten our burden.

We must therefore encourage multinational participation in

agencies for foreign aid. The United Nations is probably the best existing instrument for this purpose. Its various agencies should be supported fully and expanded, and possibly new ones should be added. Aid should be in that channel, which will result in accomplishing the most per dollar expended, and much efficient multilateral aid can be obtained through the United Nations agencies.

We are joined with other free-world countries in the International Monetary Fund to maintain exchange rates for currency stability and the promotion of trade. More recently, under American leadership the West has established The International Development Association for the purpose of providing long-term loans to underdeveloped nations. The United States at present furnishes about 40 per cent of these funds.

At the same time, we are continuing with the other advanced countries of the free world to provide long-term loans for fundamental facilities—roads, harbors, irrigation projects, and the like—that are necessary for the development of the new nations. The institution for these joint undertakings is the International Bank for Reconstruction and Development, better and more popularly known as the World Bank. Its offshoot, the International Finance Corporation, is designed to provide capital funds on a nongovernmental basis for private businesses owned by the nationals of the underdeveloped countries. These institutions draw upon the talents and resources of the entire free world and have already proved their effectiveness.

Because the essential reason for underdevelopment in the low-income countries is underutilization of physical and human resources, the General Assembly of the United Nations in 1958 established the United Nations Special Fund to carry on pre-investment activities. Its purpose is to assist the hundred low-income countries of the world in determining the potentials of their physical resources and to assist the establishment of institutes for the training of their people. Thus it is hoped that these countries can learn to make more effective use of their human and natural resources. The United Nations Special Fund, which is doing excellent work, should be financed with more adequate funds.

The United States has worked with its Latin American neighbors to establish the new billion-dollar Inter-American Development Bank, designed to support economic growth in the Americas. In 1960 the U.S. offered its Latin American neighbors a half-billion-dollar program of aid for development purposes.

WHAT ABOUT DIRECT AID, the financial aid the United States extends independently rather than jointly with other countries? We come first to the Export-Import Bank. This agency is a longtime friend of the American businessman. It makes dollar loans to foreigners who wish to buy goods in the United States. The Export-Import Bank helps stimulate our exports and is playing an increasingly important role in free-world development.

The flow of capital investment from the United States into underdeveloped areas is at a rate of about a billion dollars a year. Most of this has gone to Latin America. The less developed countries in other parts of the world are receiving little or no aid from the West. Such nations could easily use twice our present billion-dollar annual investment. For our own security if for no other reason, we must increase our unilateral investment in these areas.

We should give much positive thought to supplying more investment capital to these young, growing nations. Private rather than government capital would be best. Much of our private capital investment abroad in the past has been of the large-scale variety, largely by corporations in the oil and mining industries. There is now, however, a good opportunity for smaller ventures in manufacturing, in which U.S. companies form partnerships with local firms in those countries. Joint ownership has the advantage, among others, of demonstrating cooperation and destroying the image propagated by the Communists, that United States investment is for the purpose of exploitation. The idea of remaining free of foreign domination has strong appeal to the people in the less developed countries, especially in those new nations recently become independent. We must not overlook these psychological and sociological factors; they are important aspects of private investment abroad. An effective and lasting enterprise in a foreign land by American business requires a thorough familiarity and sympathy with the people and the conditions in the country involved.

By all odds the most important instrument of direct United States foreign aid is our successful Mutual Security Program. This includes our military assistance and defense support programs, technical cooperation, the Development Loan Fund, special assistance, and other aid programs.

The major objectives of the Mutual Security Program are the preservation of adequate defensive strength and the promotion of human betterment in the free nations of the world. Mutual Security is not a charity program, even though many of the dollars involved will never be repaid as dollars; it is an integral part of our foreign policy, indispensable to our national security and welfare.

Mutual Security is making a genuine contribution to the economic health of the United States. It helps other nations create conditions of political and economic stability and foster economic growth. When their economies are fully developed and prosperous, our friends and allies are also our best customers. The greater part of the dollars that go for either economic or military foreign aid are spent in the United States for products of United States industry.

Our criteria for allocation of aid under the Mutual Security Program must be based on need, the ability to utilize aid effectively, and the relationship of the aid extended to the security and economic strength of the free world. The advantages are reciprocal and, although in these times political considerations perhaps do play a small part, the United States does not seek to dictate to any country how it should conduct its foreign or domestic affairs.

All our foreign-aid programs must be administered in a way that will not interfere with the right of self-determination in the beneficiary nation. On the other hand, we must take care that the nations receiving aid will not become accustomed to relying upon us in every emergency. We must instead help them develop resourcefulness, political stability, competence, self-discipline, dependability, and eventually some measure of economic independence. External aid can play only a limited part in their development, because no one but they themselves can bring about that development. They must help themselves.

The rapid growth of population throughout the world presents one of the most difficult of present problems. That is because to understand it requires the longest-range forecasting of all. The number of births increases today but the number of mouths which are to be fed a reasonably adequate diet does not increase until later. Thus we fail to consider the problem difficult today, yet we know it will be immensely difficult fifteen years from now. The United States might point out to countries receiving our aid and sincerely interested in getting it that their problems cannot be solved if the population explosion around the world is to grow and aggravate the proportions of their total physical and other resources to the increasing number of their population. We could offer them assistance in population planning, and we could help them in their own understanding of the problem by pointing out the increased burdens of tomorrow represented by the increased births of today.

Many of the underdeveloped countries that are being subjected to the strongest pressure from the Communist bloc cannot meet usual banking standards for repayment terms required by most of the world's financial institutions. To backstop U.S. assistance to these countries we have established the vitally important Development Loan Fund as part of Mutual Security. The Fund stands ready to finance development projects which cannot be financed by other organizations or meet the criteria of the Export-Import Bank with its conventional bank-loan standards. The Development Loan Fund extends credit on more flexible terms to the less developed countries and may take repayment in local currency. It also places primary emphasis on financing goods and services of United States origin in making loans for development projects. Thus it also helps stimulate our export trade.

Potentially this fund offers newly developing nations an abundant hope for needed foreign capital. It is far too important to the free world to permit its operations to be slowed down or halted because of inadequate financing. We must enlarge our support of the Development Loan Fund.

The largest portion of the cost of Mutual Security goes for our military assistance program. This works on a cost-sharing basis with NATO and other allies for improvement of defense, training, and the modernization of forces with today's new and costly weapons. United States leadership in this program is developed jointly by the departments of State and Defense. The main objective is assurance of mutual defense for our allies and ourselves. It is a highly important program because it preserves the military strength of the Western World.

Also under the Mutual Security Program, the International Cooperation Administration supplies economic assistance directly related to military defense. Its defense support program is fashioned to bolster the economic resources of such countries as Korea, Formosa, and Vietnam so that maintenance of adequate defense will not be so great a strain as to cause their economies to collapse. The countries that receive defense support aid are chiefly those exposed to aggressive Communist action on the southern and eastern borders of the Sino-Soviet bloc.

The International Cooperation Administration also has highly important programs of special assistance to the less developed countries. Proceeds from the sale of surplus American commodities are used for economic development in such countries; we accept local currency for payment, and such proceeds are kept in the respective countries.

The first great premise of all our foreign-aid programs is or ought to be this: by making technical assistance steadily available in amounts Americans know they can afford, we can help developing peoples to help themselves to higher standards. Our basic objective in providing foreign aid is to help the nations of the free world develop their resources, human and natural, within the framework of a free-choice society and under leadership responsive to the wishes of the people.

No agency does more to further these ends than does the United States Technical Assistance Program of the International Cooperation Administration. Its projects in health, education, agriculture, industry, and public administration provide emerging nations and their leaders with the skills necessary for any country to grow and become self-sustaining. The activities of the ICA are carried forward by nearly 6000 people working overseas in some sixty countries on more than 2000 different projects.

It is, of course, recognized that in the past some percentage of American economic aid programs have exhibited waste and inefficiency as a result of crash government assistance programs, lack of coordination of the various agencies, and in a few cases poor administration by mediocre and untrained personnel who were uninformed about the particular country. There is a great need for a critical reappraisal of our aid, grant, and loan activities and a reorganization of the staff and program to fit the changing times and to eliminate duplication of effort. The question is how we can make our dollars get the most results in our foreign aid programs. The most qualified, understanding, and competent Americans should administer these technical assistance and other foreign-aid programs and more area nationals should be trained and employed at responsible levels. Congress can make a significant contribution in obtaining such personnel for overseas duty if it will act to insure some genuine long-term continuity in these programs. So long as the very existence of such agencies as ICA must be reauthorized each year by congressional committees, the agencies will have the greatest difficulty obtaining the best-qualified specialists. They will be unable to undertake the extensive training programs for skilled personnel that are necessary for truly effective performance overseas.

In the low-income countries, it will require long-range planning and the application of longtime remedies before self-sustaining economic growth can be attained. Up to now, our foreign-aid program to these countries has been considered temporary and short-term and the amount of its funds has been determined by annual decisions and political pressures. As a result of the insistence of Congress to review needs and appropriate funds annually, after nearly fifteen years of annual review and debating, "we are still tackling twenty-year problems with five-year plans manned by two-year personnel working with one-year appropriations." Commitments extending from three to five years should replace the annual funding of these foreign-aid programs, both U.S. and UN.

The export of able and dedicated personnel is the best contribution we can make to the development of other nations and is of key importance in the present struggle with communism. Our problem remains to find and persuade technically competent people who can win friends for freedom to live abroad for years and to acquire the necessary grasp of the language and culture of the country in which they are assigned to work.

The year 1961 marks the twelfth birthday of the technical assistance program. For more than a decade the U.S. has been extending technical knowledge and skills to underdeveloped countries. Despite the very great achievements of the past, it is now obvious that this program must go on for many more years if we are to gain our foreign-policy objectives. All of the reports on foreign aid from nongovernmental sources, such as the businessmen of the Fairless survey group, indicate that it will have to continue moving forward for a long period of time.

One effective way in which American business can help the government expand technical assistance is to loan more technical experts from its ranks to the program for work in underdeveloped countries. The government has found it difficult in the past to obtain first-rate technicians, especially from industry. Business leaders should encourage men from their companies to volunteer, and our universities and medical centers should encourage more of our talented specialists to participate actively in the technical assistance programs. Industry could help by protecting the job security and seniority rights of specialists who wish to accept government assignments and then return to private industry. Certainly it will not be impossible for businessmen to find ways to make it financially practical for technically trained men to contribute to their country's future by making their talents available to their government for a time. The minimum term overseas for technicians should be two years, preferably three. When corporations engaged in international trade send technicians overseas, they materially increase the education of those technicians. These technicians will provide permanent results only when they train nationals in the area in which they are engaged.

Carefully selected, the technicians of the free world can be the best ambassadors we have. They can convey far more than skills. They can carry at the personal-contact level to foreign lands our all-important democratic attitudes and values. We have a moral responsibility to teach and demonstrate the things in which we believe. To do this effectively, we must have a comprehensive knowledge of the attitudes, customs, values, and aspirations of the peoples of other countries so that the degree to which our ways and theirs are compatible may be fully emphasized.

THE UNITED STATES can maintain its world position of moral and material leadership only if our citizens devote the time and the effort required to understand the pressing international problems with which we are living. We cannot shirk our responsibility of knowing what is going on in the world today, nor can we shrink from giving our support to the policies that seek to implement the principles of freedom as we know and enjoy them.

The United Nations is an effective instrument for handling cooperative efforts in foreign aid, as in other matters. The UN is doing excellent work in this field, but it cannot take the place of an informed interest on the part of the American people, an interest sensitive to the needs and aspirations of other peoples.

While debate continues on what should be done about international issues, many of the needs of people as individuals seem to be glossed over. People need food, clothing, shelter. They need education. Diplomatic conversations do not increase production in a country that has a backward economy. This takes economic assistance, which only the richer countries can provide. These underdeveloped countries need the know-how, the technical equipment, and the training programs to get their people on the path toward better living.

Both government and private institutions in the United States have already spent billions to provide such aid, and will doubtless continue their programs. Help from the more favored nations to the less developed ones—beyond any humanitarian considerations—is simply good business. And it is in the national interest of the more advanced countries. It aids further widespread progress, and makes for stability in the world. Improvement elsewhere redounds to our own political and economic advantage.

But the moral consideration is the most important, and in the final analysis is the echoing reason why we must continue and improve our foreign aid: The rich and strong nations *must* help the poor and weak peoples of the world. The old words are still true: "As ye sow, so shall ye reap."

ELEVEN

ONE WORLD

EVERY ONE of the three billion people who live on earth are inhabitants of one world, and will continue to be regardless of the number of space pioneers who are placed in orbit about the earth in our lifetimes, or reach the moon. Deep in the hearts of all of us is the longing, the prayer, that the world can be without war or the threat of war—whatever our ideology, station, race. We all yearn for world peace.

World peace today would mean an end to the paralyzing threat of a third world war, the prospect of incredible and inhuman destruction. World peace would leave the future—and the present—free for the assurance of human dignity, for spiritual and artistic endeavor, for uninterrupted material progress. Lasting peace would make possible the banishment of poverty and pestilence. It would free man to realize his noblest hopes and his high destiny.

But world peace, or even the easing of the present world tensions, will not come unless we work devotedly and constantly for it. Technology does not have the answer. Harmony among nations cannot come automatically—and true harmony is more than coexistence in a kind of armed truce of two inflexibly conflicting ideologies. All members of all nations must contribute and make continuous adjustments to cope with the tensions that exist, much in the way this is done in the smaller units of the successful and happy human families. Successful families are made up of individuals who do not compromise their identities, yet they

190

are able to live in peace with each other by respecting the right to be different. Similarly, national pride and insistence on "sovereignty" must be moderated to achieve cooperation on common goals even while nations retain the right to be different as part of the right to be free. Accommodations among religious practices must be made as incompatibilities show themselves; racial antagonisms must be dampened before they explode into social convulsions; competition in trade must be consistent with fair practices. Considering these factors, peace in our time is a succession of well-managed tensions—but it is possible.

In our world there are the tensions caused by the ideology of communism opposed to the ideology of a free-choice society. Growing economic competition engenders tensions. Tensions exist between races and among religious persuasions. Especially dangerous now are the tensions between the few rich nations and the many poor countries populated by millions who will not any longer accept poverty, illiteracy, disease, and despair as inevitable for them.

Tensions, however, are not all undesirable. They can lead to constructive advances in human society. Out of tension and competition can come the stimulation for growth, the prodding for progress, and the prompting for invention. Out of the dangerous pressures that are today forced upon us we will be driven to build a better world or to destroy ourselves. The building of a better world can come as we learn to use our powers of creation and direction to manage the tensions we must face. It is not reasonable to expect or to wish to eliminate tensions; the realistic objective must be the control and guidance of the energies created by these tensions into constructive channels.

Tensions start with people, and people keep them going. The control of tensions, therefore, boils down to *people*. When we as individuals come to understand the true causes of the tensions we feel and deplore—or fear and do not understand—we can begin to do something about them. The hope that we can bring today's tensions under control is well justified in the history of mankind.

Dean Edmund Sinnott, Yale's distinguished botanist, has found in all forms of life not only infinite potentiality for improvement but also a divine purpose. Dean Sinnott traces this "directiveness" not merely through the billion years of inorganic development but through the emergence of the life-giving protoplasm as well. And in the million years since man has emerged, Dr. Sinnott sees the same purpose and direction continuously in evidence. Man's brain has slowly grown sufficiently complex for him to acquire memory, imagination, and the power of speech. With these capacities he has been able to profit by the experience of earlier generations and thus to accumulate a fund of wisdom and accelerate his progress.

From man has emerged the urge to strive, to know, to create, to struggle, to organize, to love, to cooperate. But also within his psyche remain the built-in drives that equip him to survive, to fear, to compete, to fight, to hate, to murder. All are part of the same energy. Constructive and creative impulses vie with destructive and death-dealing instincts.

Every day each individual, each family, each community must manage the encounters, the tensions, the conflicts that arise from different urges, varying wishes, divergent goals. This is the struggle of our existence, and the problems arising from tensions are inevitable. Man must therefore learn not only to live with his tensions; he must also learn to win enduring gains out of tension and struggle.

As A FIRST STEP in the reduction and control of present international tensions we must set aside the necessary time to strive for better understanding of the pressing world problems that confront all of us. A great many people in the United States are interested in learning something about other countries, especially when they expect to travel abroad, but most of us are either too busy or too little concerned to go with any depth into the problems and attitudes of people in other lands; we must therefore look beyond the seas and seek knowledge of other peoples and cultures.

Since our nation gives the most aid to the less developed countries at present and the greatest support to the United Nations, at least financially, if only as taxpayers we should all be eager to know what is being accomplished, where, and how successfully. While part of the job is to get the people of other countries to understand the United States—our people, our policies, our ideals—certainly an equally important part of the job is motivating the people of the United States to understand the cultures, needs, and aspirations of the peoples of other countries.

Much too frequently we realize, in one way or another, that too many foreigners have rather distorted views of our American way of life. These views have been gathered from the many motion pictures, books, and magazines that play up the sensational, the "interesting," the "newsworthy," rather than the constructive and more prevalent elements in our society. Our thousands of gadgets and overchromed automobiles have spread the idea that, as a nation, we are nothing but materialists. And sickening propaganda, spread by racial and religious hate groups as well as by the Communists, has done its best to augment these unfavorable false images of the United States.

Often, unintentionally, we too have contributed to this distortion. The actions of the four million Americans who live overseas or who travel abroad each year have not always given the best impression of what America really is. It is essential for our national good that those Americans who live abroad, as well as our traveling ambassadors—official and private—conduct themselves so as to win respect. Our cause will be helped immensely if these Americans will understand the people and the problems in the lands in which they reside or visit. It is likewise imperative that the vast number of our population who do not travel abroad have as full an understanding as possible of other nations.

To bring peace into the world, there must be better understanding. Everyone is afraid of the unknown. What people do not know, they tend to fear and act with hostility toward. Every nation now is beaming short-wave radio broadcasts to selected other countries in an endeavor to make direct contacts with the people of those countries.

When a crisis arises in today's world, it is vital that people abroad—particularly our friends—understand the position taken by the United States and the reasons for it. As one approach to this, we are disseminating accurate information about the United States in more than eighty nations of the free world through the United States Information Agency. USIA uses many media for telling our story to the world in terms other nations will understand. Its press service brings news to many countries, particularly in the less developed areas; its motion-picture service has the largest distribution system of any in the world; its Voice of America programs are broadcast by radio in thirty-seven different languages; and it maintains more than one hundred fifty overseas libraries. Also, in response to the world-wide interest in learning the English language, the USIA has offices throughout the world which arrange classes of instruction, seminars, and workshops for local English-language students and teachers. These English classes are attended by more than a million students.

For the past decade, Radio Free Europe, supported by voluntary contributions collected annually by the Free Europe Committee, has assisted the Voice of America by broadcasting over a privately operated chain of radio stations freedom messages and truth news to the people of the satellite countries of Europe, especially to Poland, Hungary, Czechoslovakia, Romania, and Bulgaria. These broadcasts are designed to keep up the spirits of the satellite peoples and to help them maintain courage and hope of ultimately regaining their freedom.

No SINGLE EXISTING international or supranational institution is so important to peace and understanding as the United Nations. The UN was taking shape and its charter was being drafted while World War II was still being fought. It is fortunate indeed for mankind that men of vision succeeded in founding the United Nations formally before the war fully ended. If we had waited until after the war it is more than likely that the advent of today's so-called Cold War would have prevented any workable agreement even on a charter. Had operational organization of the United Nations been delayed, even without the Cold War the tremendous scientific and social revolutions of recent years might have made it extremely difficult to bring such a complex institution into being.

The UN has two major present purposes. The first is to prevent or stop war. The second is to remove the causes of war by encouraging cooperation among nations in the economic and social areas of our life and by protecting human rights, including the right of self-determination among nations. That the UN is and can be a powerful force for peace was demonstrated many times in its first decade and a half. The United Nations was called into action in conflicts in Azerbaijan, in Korea, in the Israeli-Arab fighting, in the Suez crisis in Egypt, in Lebanon, and in the Congo upheaval.

It is a tribute to the United Nations and a hopeful sign of the mental climate of our world that it has been able to function and prevent the outbreak of a major war through the turbulent and rapidly changing years since World War II. The greatest and most powerful source of UN success is moral suasion, although perhaps the most important force in preventing war in this nuclear age lies in the fact that no nation wants to start another world war. When the risks have become great, nations on both sides of the dispute have been willing to turn to the United Nations for a solution, not to hydrogen bombs.

Lasting world peace will come as a result of a certain flexibility on the part of individuals and of nations, and by this I do not mean compromise of bedrock principle; it must be based on a willingness of all nations to seek to understand the problems and motivations of others. Therefore the UN can be no stronger than the respect of its members for the rights of each other and the willingness to listen to their points of view. The tragic history of the failure of the League of Nations must have taught us some lessons in this direction. Today, one of the great values of the United Nations is the fact that in the General Assembly it offers an open forum within which delegates of all member countries, large and small, may express their views freely. The delegates and their supporting staffs must come to know a great deal about world problems and about the people of the other member countries. But so also this must take place not only among the UN staff; it must happen among the men in the street of all the member countries.

We must strengthen the United Nations. Mankind must move from international anarchy to world order under law; to a federation of nations able to make decisions and govern the six continents; to a World Court system wherein nations will be obliged to submit their disputes; to a UN standing police agency to patrol and keep the law. While others belittle the UN and seek to weaken the structure, let us raise a banner to increase the powers of the United Nations. Let me spell out what I mean.

One of the agencies of the UN, the United Nations Educational, Scientific and Cultural Organization, is particularly active and useful in promoting education and international understanding. It seeks to encourage the free flow of persons, ideas, and information among countries. UNESCO does this by supporting scientific research and cultural interchange as well as by advancing the cause of truth, freedom, and peace throughout the world.

The United Nations as a whole and UNESCO in particular has been severely criticized in the United States by a number of individuals and organizations, including the Veterans of Foreign Wars and the Daughters of the American Revolution. The criticisms have been primarily to the effect that UNESCO was "subversive" and advocated world government as well as atheism. I believe that these charges were based on misinformation, sometimes on the unwillingness to understand, and on the unfounded fear that the activities of UNESCO would infringe on our national sovereignty—which they do not.

Education has emerged as the highest-priority problem in the countries that have recently gained independence. International cooperation in the education of people all over the world in science, the humanities, and the arts should be recognized as being of the utmost importance to international understanding. Because of this world-wide need for progress in education we should support UNESCO wholeheartedly.

If the whole UN is to survive as an entity, it must grow stronger and be allowed to operate with increasing effectiveness. If it is to fulfill the functions for which it was created, it must have powers of enforcement recognized and respected by all the nations of the world. The UN will grow stronger only if the member nations accept and fulfill their obligations to it. This is especially true of the United States and the other great powers, who must assume heaviest responsibility for support and unselfish leadership. Otherwise the UN will wither from neglect to the point it can be destroyed by vicious attacks from those who would choose war and conquest as the means to attain the power for which they hunger.

For several months before the failure of the big-power summit meeting in Paris in 1960, for example, the UN was being bypassed in the relations among the great nations. The big powers planned a summit conference outside the frame of reference of the UN; they had set up their own disarmament negotiations. Then suddenly the summit meeting collapsed and the Congo crisis exploded; the Security Council was in session literally night and day; everything again focused on UN action and decisions.

If the major powers treat the UN merely as a diplomatic tool, to be used when they choose and neglected when they please, it cannot succeed. On the other hand, if the members—particularly the powerful nations—make the UN the foundation of their policies of dealing with the relationships among nations and at the same time strive honestly to strengthen world cooperation and organization, the UN will indeed be a success and will grow desirably stronger each time it weathers a crisis.

From the point of view of the United States today, the most constructive way for us to meet the difficulties that seem the stock in trade of the Communist bloc is through the channel of a strong and vigorous United Nations. In the Security Council, and even more in the General Assembly, we can work to win the majority of nations for freedom and justice, and this is what is needed: the honoring of freedom and justice for all, not a rubber-stamp agreement every time with our point of view. If we work patiently and diligently and unceasingly in the UN, member nations, particularly the new states, can come to realize that we are acting for their benefit as well as for our own. And such an awareness by the other member nations will make it increasingly difficult for the Communists to stir up dissension.

The United Nations also offers the great advantage of being a clearing-house in providing assistance to the less developed regions of the world. Much has been done, but much more needs to be done. The UN needs to strengthen and enlarge the work of its agencies and programs of assistance to the less fortunate. This would include the technical assistance program, the Special Fund, the World Bank, and the International Development Association. Through these programs the UN can assist its new member nations in the preparation of development plans for their countries. This economic research and planning can be accomplished by experts and technicians supplied by the UN and recruited from all the nations who have such personnel. It is amazing how much a few skilled engineers, technicians, and other specialists can do to decrease tensions and help stabilize potentially dangerous situations.

We must strengthen the United Nations or be prepared to supplant the present United Nations with another world body which will accomplish the worthy objectives of the UN. In order to have a responsible world social order in which wealth and opportunity are more fairly shared, there must be some kind of permanent legislative organization which seeks to maintain peace and which builds up conditions that promote the world's general welfare.

We Americans should favor giving the United Nations a greater degree of effective authority. The problem of outer space offers one good reason for this. No single nation should be permitted to try to lay claim to outer space or any segment of it. Authority for the exploration of space should be vested in the UN. Similarly, the United Nations should have wider control over the development and uses of nuclear energy. A world-wide program of atoms for peace, not bombs, is indeed appropriate. Eventually the United Nations should be in a position to control world-wide disarmament. It should supervise a global system of justice and law, and it should maintain a permanent security force powerful enough to stop the terrible waste of war.

THE WORD *neighbor* is rapidly taking on new dimensions in our modern world. It is gathering growing significance through improving communications, ever-increasing economic interdependence (whether we seek this or not), and through the need to close ranks against the enemies of freedom. Slowly but inevitably human beings everywhere are beginning to realize that we must all live in the world together, and that we must permit the opportunity for others to achieve the same dignity and rights we want for ourselves.

In the shrinking world of today we are beginning slowly to comprehend the divine principle that mankind is a brotherhood; that we *are* all our brothers' keepers, whatever differences may exist between nations, races, and creeds. In his book *The Phenomenon of Man* Pierre Teilhard de Chardin has pointed out that an exploding population, in combination with contemporary trade and communications, has covered the earth with a continuous blanket of mankind. He speculates that we are participants in a new stage of human evolution and that we shall emerge from this stage with a new kind of human species which will be as far in advance of what we are now as twentieth-century man is different from Neanderthal man.

And what will be the primary benefit of this further evolution? Chardin describes it as a new relationship in which every nation will be a part of a world body politic, and every individual will realize he is a cell in the world mind. The evolutionary maturity of men and women in the future will be marked by their successful interaction with all other human beings. Different people of every race, nation, and religion will be members of a world body, one of another, much as hands and feet, eyes and ears, are organs or appendages of a single coordinate body.

To hasten the realization of this bright future and to find the answer to the widespread prayer for world peace, we will need universal communication in an open world in which nothing interferes with the free exchange and evaluation of ideas. We will need an equitable measure of economic development and material well-being for all peoples. We will need a much stronger United Nations, assuring justice and rule of law maintained by a World Court, and an effective police system. This must come for the whole planet—and beyond.

The goal of One World is worthy of our greatest striving, our highest abilities, and our noblest potential. It is a common destiny to which each and all of mankind can contribute. Peace with justice and freedom through world order and under universal law is attainable. Let us work for it.

TWELVE

RAISING A STANDARD

IN THIS BOOK I have tried to bring into focus and to sum up what I believe to be the high road the American people must follow into the future. I have endeavored at least to suggest the paths we must walk to meet the great challenges of our time, not merely for our own survival as individuals or even as a nation but for the survival of the whole family of man.

But recognition of existing challenges, and even high-principled resolution to face them, is of no avail unless we take action. We must therefore begin to do what must be done; we must begin with a united faith in ourselves and in our beliefs and traditions that is reinforced by ability and willingness to work out specific plans and practical measures for the accomplishment of the objectives we already have and the further ones we must set.

Our best objectives for tomorrow are based upon a fundamental and unshakable belief in the potentialities of human beings—each human being and all mankind—the growing edge of creative evolution. This belief stems from the principle that we are more than ourselves, that (however we express it) we realize that we are expressions of a divine spirit. In our generation man has gained fantastic knowledge and accumulated vast powers to fashion and utilize our physical environment. My faith in a divine order leads me to the optimistic belief that man will use these powers for good. We are beginning to realize that man has vastly greater potential than he has developed so far.

With only a tiny fraction of the attention and resources he has expended upon learning how to control his physical environment, man can release and profit from great powers within himself that will direct the energy of the atom.

This faith in human potentialities for good is the basis for belief in freedom. Democracy is more than a form of government: it is a way of life. Otherwise there can be no answer to Jefferson's question: If people cannot be trusted to govern themselves, how then can they be trusted to govern others? Democracy makes it possible for people to develop their capacities by permitting the exercise of those capacities—by making choices, and abiding by and learning from the consequences.

Freedom is indivisible in the pursuits of life. The liberty to worship, think, speak, listen, read, publish, vote, and assemble, and the freedoms to choose one's work and to use one's money are all inseparable. Freedom must encompass the whole of life or eventually it will exist in no part of that life. Freedom in one area buttresses freedom in others; restrictions or denials in one aspect of life threaten freedom in some other aspect. One of our tasks today is to learn and relearn that freedom is a thing of unity, of oneness. We must emphasize the wholeness of freedom and its alternative. We must be vigilant against those who would be zealous in their concern for freedom in some special area— the intellect, politics, or economics—and indifferent to it in other areas.

Freedom is indivisible in the human race. The enslavement of a people in one country is a threat to the freedom of people in every other part of the world. Lincoln understood this clearly when he abolished slavery in the United States a century ago; we should see it clearly in the world in which we live, today. The gifted and energetic but enslaved peoples of continental China, the Soviet Union, and Hungary, for example, are mobilized against free men and women in the United States and the rest of the free world. Poverty and disease are also enslavement. The lack of adequate preparation for freedom in countries such as the Congo is a danger to the peace of the entire world; freedom requires both training and awareness. The denial of full rights to certain racial or religious groups in the United States is a threat to the freedom of all groups. We dare not be indifferent to the loss of freedom by *any* group in our own country or in any other part of the world.

Mankind's search for freedom cannot now be considered apart from the United States of America. Since the Declaration of Independence, the American experiment has had meaning for the entire human race. Its principles and precepts, enunciated nearly two centuries ago, are not restricted to time or place; they are part of the best of the human spirit. These principles made clear that all men shall have equal opportunity to develop their native capacities, that they have certain inalienable rights, and that to secure these rights government shall be instituted among men. So long as these ideals are imperfectly realized anywhere on earth—including within our own borders—the American Revolution is unfinished.

A quick review of world history since 1776 attests the universal relevance of the ideals that found expression in the documents of the American Revolution. The best of the French Declaration of the Rights of Man took inspiration from the American Declaration. Great Britain, at home and in the development of the Commonwealth of Nations, has been guided by lessons learned from the American War for Independence. The wars for independence in Latin America and the liberal revolutions in Europe in the nineteenth century looked to the North American example. New nations that have emerged since World War II have copied, sometimes perhaps rather imperfectly, the American pattern.

Even the Communists pay the American experiment a kind of back-handed compliment. The Communists claim to be for the twentieth century what the American Revolution was for the eighteenth and nineteenth. The claim is false, of course, at the very core. Communism is a blueprint for a *finished* revolution. Even before it is begun, the Communist plan freezes the mold and excludes all methods of peaceful revision. Communism is a blueprint for a *dogmatic* revolution, without any adjustment or regard for culture or history. Yet, because the people of the United States have relaxed in their devotion to the universal implication of their experiment, this spurious substitute has enslaved and still bewitches many of the peoples of the earth.

WE CAN, AND WE MUST, renew our faith in our great tradition and in the everlasting principles of human freedom. We can help the cause of freedom in at least two ways:

We can first demonstrate that freedom *works* in the United States. We must push unfalteringly onward toward the goal of giving all our own people the full exercise of their inalienable rights to life, liberty, and the pursuit of happiness. We must expand opportunities for the less fortunate and press on to seek new and higher goals for all Americans. Freedom of choice may well become more rather than less difficult as the future becomes the present. Yet in these new choices are the new frontiers of the human spirit.

The second way we can and must assist the cause of freedom is by helping other peoples and nations in every way open to us. We must help these people to enter an age of science in which science is applied to the attainment of human well-being. Bread must precede lectures to those who are hungry, yet we must win the underdeveloped and uncommitted nations for freedom. Establishing freedom is more difficult than achieving the aims of communism. *We* must win by the rules of the game, by persuasion. The Communists want only to create confusion where they cannot dominate, to achieve dominance where they can, and to maintain domination where they have won. Our goal is to help people advance for their own purposes and according to their own lights, no matter at what stage they now are. This means dealing with highly sophisticated and advanced peoples; it also means helping highly sophisticated cultures that have underdeveloped economies, as in India and Burma. And it means giving of our skills, possessions, and good will to help such elementary peoples as the Congolese. The task is great, but freedom hangs in the balance.

Americans today need to be particularly concerned about the widening gap between the underdeveloped and the highly advanced economies of the world. Everybody now seems to be moving ahead, but some travel by oxcart and some by airplane. So that, although the movement is forward, the differences between rich and poor nations are nevertheless growing larger. The first impact of an advanced technology on an underdeveloped economy may be a lower, not a higher, standard of living. Improved health and medical aid brings the death rate down, and total population increases. For economic growth, goods and services are drawn from current consumption and put into capital investment. Hence the appeal of the Communist system for "short cuts" and the trend toward authoritarian government in some parts of the world. The appeal of communism is indeed false; totalitarian governments have no short cuts save the firing squad. But the American people must recognize the urgency of the problem. We must sympathize with the impatience of the underdeveloped nations, so like our own in our early days, and help make the transition from poverty to plenty as quick and smooth as possible.

How CAN AMERICANS HELP the underdeveloped peoples of the world? How can we win them for freedom? These are really one question. The answer can be summed up in two words: *productivity* and *concern*. Productivity is the key to the plenty that gives our people the margin above subsistence to pursue goals beyond survival—to demonstrate the advantages of freedom, to defend it, and to help others throughout the world to be free.

Concern, in the sense the Quakers use the word, is a regard for the worth of all people everywhere and the desire to help them, not because they are "useful" but simply because they are fellow human beings. If we have concern we shall use of our abundance to bring bread and freedom to the less fortunate in the world and we shall do this because it is the right thing to do.

Our first task should be to raise some flags for new ideas great enough for these new times. One is the need, in an era when a "cosmonaut" can encircle the earth in 108 minutes, for a UN world security force. Because this idea will take time to percolate and gain acceptance, NATO, SEATO, and America must realistically maintain military strength, whatever the cost, until such time as the burden of armament can safely be reduced. This must at least now remain our paramount consideration, not alone for ourselves but also for our allies and for the many defenseless peoples coming into nationhood who can be free only so long as we are strong.

At the same time it is essential that we expand the economic strength of our country by increasing the rate of our industrial growth. This will make our armament burden lighter, and the enlarged output of goods and services will also permit us to extend more aid to the nations overseas. In vigorously expanding industrial production, we must use government stimulation only to the extent to which it encourages but does not replace individual initiative. In our race to establish freedom abroad we must not lose our economic freedom at home.

One all-important prerequisite to enlarging our economic power is the maintenance of a sound and stable currency. When other nations prefer our gold to our credit, it is a warning that we cannot afford to be profligate in the use of our financial resources. To preserve the strength of the dollar we must keep our federal budget in balance and hold the line on inflation. We must also insist that other prosperous nations of the free world share equitably in the burden of aid to underdeveloped areas. And we must increase our exports.

Our strength in the future must come from its source in the past: millions of individual Americans working hard and co-ordinating their efforts for the common good. We must stay firmly with the basic principles upon which our great nation was built and we cannot afford *ever* to relax our efforts to put these principles to use always more fruitfully. This challenge must be met by more than words. It will take a united, understanding population imbued with these tested ideals, striving—whatever the personal sacrifice—to effect them.

America must continue to be the land of opportunity encouraging business enterprise, with abundant job possibilities, high wages, fair profits and rewards, and with checks and balances to assure a just range between the less rich and the more rich. We need leaders in both business and labor with a keen sense of social responsibility based on the realization that in our economic life we are all interdependent—management, labor, stockholders, and the consuming public. While each of us is free, in our system, to choose his own career, to work at the job he wants, to purchase what he wants with his money, and to lead his life in his own way, none of us is self-sufficient. Without the services of others it would be impossible to survive as well, and difficult to survive at all.

We must strengthen our educational institutions so as to afford a better education to all, with provision for the unusually gifted to develop their talents. Education is the foundation of democracy; man must have knowledge if he is to govern himself wisely, and education offers opportunity. It satisfies the universal urge of man toward self-realization; at the same time, it recognizes the unique character of the individual. The democracies cannot afford to ride on past pedagogical laurels: ours is not the only political system that allows the individual the opportunity to develop fully according to his natural endowment. Russians with special talents are paid to develop intellectual endowments to fullest capacity. China is erecting a school and university system superior to anything that country had before communism.

To defeat organized tyranny in the world we must continue to achieve a more highly educated society and preserve its freedom of inquiry and expression. Our educational institutions must endeavor to be of greater assistance in promoting understanding of our international problems, because such understanding is today an absolute essential.

Democracy is enormously more than a form of government. An expression of the human spirit at its best, some of democracy can be written into law, but its essence is in such attitudes as tolerance and fraternity and such processes as discussion and cooperation. The method of democracy is to rely on the collective judgment of a well-informed citizenry. It represents, as Abraham Lincoln put it, "patient confidence in the ultimate justice of the people."

From the beginning Americans have subscribed heartily to the philosophy that our government exists to serve the people. Too many of us just as heartily demand more and more services from government, ignoring that part of our credo which holds that government should do for the people only those things the people cannot do for themselves. We must always remember that more services mean bigger government, more control, higher costs, and heavier taxes. Taxes, as I have pointed out before, now take a quarter of our gross national production, and costs are mounting at all levels of government. Such expenditures by the state will have to be restrained if we are to maintain and improve our economic health. Every government spending proposal must be weighed carefully against its true cost—the burden it places on our free-enterprise system. In education, old-age care, housing, transportation, mail, military defense, agriculture subvention, the United States Congress has socialized our economy to some extent. Medical care is under discussion. How far do we wish to go? Some men predict that the evolution of communism will be toward more forms of capitalism, and changes in the free-choice economies will include further advances into socialism. Have we reached a point at which it would be dangerous both to the safety of our freedom and to our economic strength to permit government to encroach much farther on our private economic lives?

Men and women all over the world have a single goal in common—a better standard of living. Yet more than a third of them live in poverty and disease and have little hope of improving their situation without aid and guidance from outside. The challenge to the free and rich countries of the world is to provide such aid and guidance fast enough so that these presently less fortunate nations will choose the path to freedom rather than the dead-end road to communism. This challenge is intensified by the growing economic power of the Soviet bloc and the willingness of the Communists to use aid, trade, and technical assistance to further their aim of world conquest.

We have no choice, therefore, than to help the less fortunate people of the world. Greater economic well-being can best be accomplished through the development of their own resources, their technical skills, and their basic abilities. We must educate and train at the same moment we extend dollars and goods. We must hold before the attention of those less fortunate the realizable hope of building for themselves a society with freedom and responsible government as its guiding principles. And with our help must go understanding. As a nation that struggled from a colonial beginning, we should be able to understand the aspirations of other nations with similar beginnings. We must realize, however, that many of the newer nations at the same time have old cultures and customs which may require different approaches to their own development.

In this age we must nurture the values and traditions of the Western world. But we must also learn to appreciate the philosophies and cultures of other nations. Indeed, there are spiritual insights comprehended by Asians and Africans that can help us guard our freedom. We must remember that so long as freedom is kept, it is indivisible and can suffer no encroachment. The preservation of freedom for ourselves and the extension of freedom to others is the heart of our national purpose; it is the only way in which we can keep freedom for ourselves.

We must also make every reasonable and sincere effort to cultivate understanding, trust, and good will with the human beings who are in the Communist-controlled nations. This is a moral imperative, for in our religious belief they are as much children of God as we are. At the same time, we must be tough-minded and not allow ourselves to be misled. Moreover, while we guard our vital world-wide interests, we must abstain from words and acts that would invite war, because not to do so would mean the end of civilization. Military preparedness but not war must be accompanied by alert and constantly fresh ideas in diplomacy and foreign policy.

CAN WE SUCCEED in our undertaking? Yes, if we are willing to pay the price.

I believe that the free world has the ability, the vision, and

the determination to organize its vast material and human resources and to coordinate its efforts to extend the ideals of freedom and abundance to all the peoples of the world. And I believe that other nations, if they accept the fundamentals of a
free-choice society, can apply its principles in their own way.
It is at once our privilege and our duty to keep the banner of
freedom raised high. There is now no alternative.

I believe that as individuals and as a nation we must be ready,
able, and willing to adjust constantly to changes both at home
and abroad without compromising our basic principles of freedom. I believe we shall move forward with positive thinking
toward positive goals. This simple philosophy has long strengthened my faith in mankind. It is reinforced by my experience.
I have observed that people have infinite courage to overcome
adversity and that this is coupled with an infinite capacity for
doing good. The courage to overcome adversity springs from
an abiding faith in an Almighty power. Faith in ourselves stems
also from faith in the Creator of whom we are expressions, parts.
Free and courageous people, endowed by the vital spiritual
energy of the universe, we can determine our own destiny as
individuals and as a nation.

The purpose of America in the years ahead of us must be
immeasurably greater than simply winning the race with the
Communists, although that must not for an instant be under-
estimated. More than a century and a half ago, at his first
inaugural, George Washington stated our purpose:

Let us raise a standard to which the wise and the honest can repair.
The event is in the hand of God.

That purpose has not changed.

It is right and proper today, perhaps more than ever before
in the history of man's struggle upward, to raise this standard.
In support of it we must do more than affirm or reaffirm our

faith. We must work to bring freedom and justice to men and women everywhere—*and* improve their material well-being. We must, and we can, demonstrate the almost incredible benefits and potential of our way of life so clearly that even those who now oppose us will eventually join us in a peaceful progress that embraces all mankind.

ABOUT THE AUTHOR

Harry A. Bullis was born on October 7, 1890, in Hastings, Nebraska. The family later moved to Council Bluffs, Iowa, where young Bullis took on a paper route for the Council Bluffs, Iowa, *Nonpareil*. At prep school and at the University of Wisconsin, where he majored in economics, Mr. Bullis paid his expenses by working in a variety of jobs—operating a boarding club, as an assistant electrician, and wholesaling sewing machines. After graduation, he went to the Chase National Bank in New York as assistant to a vice president. He enlisted as an Army private in World War I, and acquired captain's bars after eighteen months overseas.

After the war, Mr. Bullis sought a broader horizon than he found in banking. He learned that the Washburn Crosby Company—a flour-milling firm—was looking for men. He went to Minneapolis in 1919 and obtained a job there as a mill employee. After a year, he was transferred to the company's general office. Some eight years later, Washburn Crosby Company was enlarged into a new corporation called General Mills, and Mr. Bullis was named secretary and comptroller. In December, 1942, he was named president.

On January 1, 1948, Harry A. Bullis became Chairman of the Board of General Mills. Eleven years later, he retired; but he continues with the corporation as a member of the Board of Directors.

Honors have come to Mr. Bullis from many directions. He has been awarded eleven honorary doctorate degrees, and is an acknowledged authority on economic and political affairs. He was named a National Association of Manufacturers "Man of the Year" in 1953, and in 1957 received the Free Enterprise Awards Association "American Success Story" plaque. He served for twelve years as an officer or director of the United States Chamber of Commerce and for a number of years as chairman of its Committee on Economic Policy. Business and educational groups, civic organizations and branches of the federal government have called upon him for his services.

DATE DUE

JAN 13 1999			
GAYLORD			PRINTED IN U.S.A.